BEYOND PERSUASION

HOW TO RECOGNISE AND USE DARK PSYCHOLOGY, NEURO-LINGUISTIC PROGRAMMING, AND MIND CONTROL IN EVERYDAY LIFE

REBECCA DOLTON

CONTENTS

The 12-step process of Brainwashing

This checklist includes:

- The 12 steps of Brainwashing as proposed by Robert Lifton, a researcher working with American prisoners of war.
- How you can spot similar tactics that are sometimes used in destructive personal relationships.

This is an excerpt from Beyond Persuasion, to receive your 12 – step brainwashing checklist, scan the QR code below:

BEYOND PERSUASION

HOW TO RECOGNISE AND USE DARK PSYCHOLOGY, NEURO-LINGUISTIC PROGRAMMING, AND MIND CONTROL IN EVERYDAY LIFE

Rebecca Dolton

INTRODUCTION

Do you ever find yourself doing something against your better judgment? Did you once have a strong opinion about something, only to find yourself swayed to believe differently? If so, you've experienced a psychological trick called 'manipulation.'

Manipulation is a loaded word. For most people, it comes with very negative connotations. It conjures images of abusive lovers, toxic parents, con artists, and sleazy lawyers.

But manipulation isn't always bad. Have you ever tried to convince someone you love to stop smoking? Or a stubborn relative to consent to a life-saving surgery? Believe it or not, these kinds of situations are also considered manipulation Businesspeople and politicians do it all day long in their professions. So do hostage negotiators, elementary school teachers, and small business owners. Advertising is an entire industry that runs on manipulation. Artists use manipulation to make you believe the word on a theatre stage is real, or that a particular character in a novel is a hero or a villain.

Whether it's used for good or bad, right or wrong, manipulation is simply the art of persuasion. While it may sound insidious, manipulation is at the core of many human social behaviours and rituals. Most of our interpersonal communications, both verbal and nonverbal, are based on manipulative strategies, and for the most part, it's good for us. Manipulation saves us from painful fights, unnecessary conflict, and hurtful words. Paradoxically, manipulation tactics often strengthen our trust in people and improve our ability to communicate with others. The trouble comes, of course, when the other person doesn't have your best intentions in mind. When someone is manipulating you for purposes of power and control, it can be tough to detect until it's too late.

That's where this book comes in. Consider this your all-purpose guide to manipulation, whether it's the beneficial tactics of persuasion and negotiation or the harmful strategies of mind control and brainwashing.

This book will walk you through manipulation in all its forms, good and bad. It will give you all the guidance you need to determine what kinds of manipulation the people around you are using and walk you through simple strategies you can use to defend yourself against those who seek to harm or control you.

This book will also provide you with strategies you can use yourself, in both personal and professional settings, to become a more sophisticated negotiator. Manipulation, or persuasion, is the backbone of negotiation. We are continually negotiating, whether we're debating which restaurant to eat at this weekend or trying to close a significant deal with a rival corporation. This book will walk you through persuasive tactics you can use to improve your personal and professional relationships, teaching you how to get what you want from other people without continually having to fight for it. It will also teach you ways to combat those who are seeking to manipulate you.

Though it may sound counter-intuitive, people are often more willing to give you what you want when you don't say it directly. There are times when it's better to be blunt, but as a good negotiator, you will be able to read the other person, understanding what to say and when to convince them to do what it is you want. After practising the strategies outlined in this book, you may be pleasantly surprised to find how much more willing people are to do as you ask, and with a lot less effort on your part!

But perhaps you're the opposite kind of person. Perhaps you find yourself quickly silenced by other people. You often feel pushed around or trampled over. Perhaps you have very strong-willed people in your family or workplace. Maybe you always find yourself being pushed around by your friends or partner. This book will show you exactly how to get what you want, no matter what situations or personalities you may have in front of you. No longer will you have to submit to the bullying of other people. Instead, you'll have a tool kit of effective strategies to persuade and convince even the most influential personalities to bend to your will.

By the end of this book, you'll be a more confident communicator in all areas of your life. You'll have all the tools to handle difficult and dangerous people in the future. You'll be able to successfully steer your way out of toxic relationships, spot the warning signs of dark psychology before it's too late, and navigate even the most volatile interpersonal situations. Manipulation will help you to get what you want out of life without continually butting heads with the people you love. It will help you to achieve success with other people smoothly and efficiently. Understanding manipulation is understanding communication at its most sophisticated. You'll begin to see all how the people around you have been manipulating you, and you'll know what you can do to take back control of your life and your relationships.

Many of the strategies in this book will take some practice before they start to work for you, but the knowledge you gain will be immediate. No matter what you want, there is a way to get it. And no matter what someone else wants from you, there is a way to resist without compromising your dignity or your safety. If you're ready to achieve full autonomy in every relationship truly, simply turn the page to learn the truth about all human communications.

1

MANIPULATION VS PERSUASION

'Manipulation' is a loaded word. Even the dictionary assigns multiple meanings to this one word. The older definition simply reads "using something, often with a lot of skill." If you manipulate machinery or data, you're regarded as someone who is highly talented, even praiseworthy (Cambridge Dictionary, 2020).

But if you manipulate a person, that's rarely understood to be a good thing. The first definition that appears in the Cambridge English Dictionary for 'manipulation' reads "controlling someone or something to your advantage, often unfairly or dishonestly" (Cambridge Dictionary, 2020). It's the last part of that definition that's critical to understanding manipulation. Especially when we talk about interpersonal relationships, manipulation almost always means using subtle communicative tactics to control another person for your gain. Manipulation is carried out for selfish reasons, often to harm another person. If you're seeking to control, dominate, or take advantage of someone, then you're using manipulation (Simon, 2010).

But what if you're a surgeon trying to convince a reluctant patient to consent to a surgery that might save their life? You may use the same tactics that a serial killer uses to lure in a victim, or that an abusive husband uses to gaslight his wife. The style of communication is nearly identical. In essence, you are manipulating your patient. But when it comes to communication, intention counts for quite a lot. Because there is a distinct difference between a concerned doctor and serial killer, a new word has entered common parlance to distinguish the two types of communication. That word is 'persuasion.' More and more often, this word has appeared in as varied places as business manuals, hostage negotiation courses, and self-help books (Cialdini, 1984).

Persuasion and manipulation are two sides of the same coin. They both refer to employing subtle communication strategies to convince someone else to do what you want. When these tactics are employed to harm another person, it's called a manipulation. When these tactics are employed with the intention of either helping another person or for gaining a personal advantage that will not harm the other party, it's called persuasion (Cialdini, 1984).

This book is intended to help you recognise and master these communication tactics in all their forms, both light and dark. When speaking about tactics that are used to harm and control others, the word manipulation will be used. When speaking about tactics that are used to get the results you want out of personal or professional situations, the word persuasion will be used.

As you read through this book, you may find that the line between manipulation and persuasion is blurry at best. You may find similar patterns appearing as you move from chapter to chapter. The suave abuser, the savvy businessman, and the teacher that's "really good" with kids will all start to look very similar, and that's ok! The teacher and the abuser both understand the same truths about human psychology. They understand how our brains work and use that knowledge to convince other people to think and behave in specific ways. The difference, of course, is that the teacher is using these truths to help teach young children right from wrong. She uses these truths to manage behaviour in her classroom and convince her students to participate in their learning. The abuser, on the other hand, uses these truths only for themselves. They apply their knowledge to make their partner fear things that aren't there, believe things that aren't true, and doubt things that they once took for granted. You will learn these truths as well, but how you decide to use them is up to you.

If the line is still a bit fuzzy, there are a few things to watch for when you suspect someone may be using manipulative or persuasive tactics. The first is the presence of sadism (Cooper, 2019). This is the intention of inflicting pain on another person, whether that pain is physical, psychological, or even sexual. Persuasion is never done to inflict unnecessary pain.

The second warning sign is selfishness (Cooper, 2019). Imagine that you and your partner are trying to decide which restaurant to go to this weekend. You want to go to the new Chinese restaurant in town, but you know your partner is reluctant because it's a bit upscale, and they are cautious about how they spend their money. If you know spending their money in this way will cause them some kind of distress, but you employ psychological tactics to convince them anyway, then you are manipulative. You know that it's against the other person's best interests to do as you wish, but you don't care. However, if you understood that your partner's unwillingness is due to something inconsequential, such as laziness or unwillingness to try something new, then convincing him to go to the new restaurant isn't manipulation, it's persuasion. In this situation, you are not putting someone in distress for your gain; you're merely negotiating for what you want.

The third, but perhaps most crucial warning sign of manipulative behaviour is malevolence (Cooper, 2019). This is the intent of harming another person for the sake of it. Whether you think it's just good fun, you're looking for revenge, or you're seeking to gain some kind of power over the other person, the intent to harm another without any feelings of remorse puts you firmly in the territory of manipulation.

A BRIEF HISTORY OF MANIPULATION

The communication tactics we now call manipulation and persuasion have been employed by humans throughout our history, but the study of these tactics from a psychological perspective is relatively recent. It began in the 1950s with the theory of social influence or how humans change their behaviours in response to specific social stimuli. One of the pioneers in this field of research was a Harvard professor named Herbert Kelman. Kelman was primarily focused on people's responses. In X situation, how do people react? What if you put the same person in a different situation? We know that not everyone reacts the same way to the same social situations, so what creates the difference? Is it personality? Previous experiences?

Kelman put people's reactions into three broad categories: compliance, identification, and internalisation (Kelman, 1958). Compliance is when someone does what another person wants them to do, but inside, they don't want to do it. Perhaps they even make it clear to the other person that they don't want to do it. Compliance is what we do when our boss assigns us to a challenging project or when our teacher gives us homework over the weekend. We don't want to do it, but we do it anyway. Compliance is what happens when someone's authority over us influences our behaviour. That authority may come in the form of power, such as a teacher or boss, or in the form of fear, such as from someone who is bigger than us or someone we know will do us harm if we don't do as they wish (Kelman, 1958).

One of the fundamental experiments in psychology pertaining to obedience is the Milgram Experiment. Stanley Milgram was trying to understand how ordinary people, when thrown into war and made to be soldiers, could perform such heinous acts against humanity despite not having a prior history of violence. His experiment places subjects in a room with a figure of authority – the experimenter – and a machine designed to give shocks to another man in the adjacent room if he should answer some questions wrongly. The voltage of shocks increased with every wrong answer, and the subject was informed that the highest voltage was enough to kill a man. Despite pleas for help and to stop the experiment from the man in the adjacent room, an actor obviously, most subjects continued the experiment until the actor went ominously quiet. They continued because the experimenter in the room took the responsibility of whatever happened to the man receiving the shocks (Milgram, 1963). This gives us a glimpse into the power authority holds over most of us – we're easily willing to turn a blind eye to the distress of someone because an alleged higher authority took responsibility for our actions.

Identification, on the other hand, is when we are influenced to change our behaviour from a place of respect (Kelman, 1958). Perhaps as a teenager, you cut your hair or changed your style of dress to look more like a celebrity you admired. Perhaps as an adult, you find yourself trying new foods because of a particular Instagram feed that you follow. We are influenced to change our behaviour because we want to be more like someone that we admire and respect, or even because we want someone that we admire and respect to like us (Kelman, 1958).

Finally, there is internalisation. Internalisation happens when both our behaviours and our beliefs are changed as a direct response to someone else's influence (Kelman, 1958). Advertising campaigns, political rallies, and religious doctrines are all based on the concept of internalisation. It's what happens when our behaviours become part of our identities. For example, perhaps your parents told you over and over again that a good parent provides for their family. When you have your own family as an adult, you'll look for the job that pays the most to keep your family as financially comfortable as possible, perhaps even giving up on specific career paths that may not have promised as much monetarily. In this case, you've internalised the advice you got from your parents. Their influence has not just changed your behaviour; it changed your worldview. It changed how you view yourself and your place in the world (Kelman, 1958).

The most successful manipulators and persuaders achieve internalisation in their targets, but even compliance is still a success. Getting someone to do something that they don't want to do when you think about it is quite an amazing feat. But we, as humans, comply all the time. You might drive three hours to have Thanksgiving at your relative's house when you don't even *like* your relative that much. You put kale in your salad because your doctor said it was good for you. You get blue curtains because your partner liked them, even though you wanted the gold ones. We comply with others several times a day, every single day, and we fool ourselves into thinking that we're the ones in control. But these decisions, more often than not, are based on subtle communication dynamics that the people around us employ all the time. And whether or not we realise it, we're doing the same to the people around us.

So, what convinces people to conform to the wishes of others? What causes us to be influenced by certain people while dominant over others? Morton Deutsch and Harold Gerard were a research pair that determined how and why humans are influenced. Primarily, we all find ourselves conforming to the expectations of others to fulfil two basic psychological needs: the need to be right (what Deutsch and Gerard called "informational social influence") and the need to be liked (what Deutsch and Gerard called "normative social influence") (Deutsch & Gerard, 1955).

If you can make the other person believe that doing what you want them to do makes them 'right' somehow, whether that means they have more knowledge, skill, talent, etc., then they'll do (or even think) just about whatever you want them to. And if that doesn't work, making the other person believe that you (and/or others) will like, love, respect, or even accept them if they do as you wish, then the results are the same. Whether you're dealing with a rival CEO or a psychotic killer holding ten people hostage, these two core psychological needs are the buttons that you need to push if you wish to influence them to change their behaviour. And though we all like to believe we're more sophisticated than this, the reality is that every time you're influenced to change your behaviour, it's because someone else has promised to fulfil those basic needs for you.

IS EVERYONE MANIPULATIVE?

The truth is that everyone is practising social influence in every social situation. Sometimes we're influencing, and other times we're being influenced, but the subtle forces of influence are present in all of our relationships. This may seem frightening, but the social influence is what holds our society and our relationships together. Without it, we'd be incapable of compromise. Even master manipulators find themselves persuaded to buy a well-placed product in the check-out line, vote a certain way by the rousing words of a political leader, or drive three hours to have Thanksgiving with some family members. Our brains are wired to both influence and be influenced. It's the primary way that we form community and build identity. In the form of persuasion, social influence is how our parents teach us right from wrong and how married couples happily live together for decades. Its how laws are written and dismantled. It's how all of our social institutions, from hospitals to the music industry to the stock market, can grow and thrive year after year.

But if you divide social influence into the categories of manipulation and persuasion, then not everyone is manipulative. At least, not all the time. Every so often, all of us find ourselves trying to convince someone to do something for us that we know isn't good for them. Did you ever try to convince your parents to lend you the car when you were a teenager? Or cajole your little brother into letting you have the largest slice of pizza *and* the last glass of Pepsi?

But truly manipulative people are those who manipulate all the time. It's when the rules of social influence are used by someone to do repeated harm to others that manipulation changes from something necessary and natural to something very dark indeed. The sophisticated use of social influence to harm is what most contemporary psychologists and cognitive-behavioural scientists are referring to when they talk about manipulation. While everyone is practising social influence, not everyone is manipulative. At least, not in a chronic and deeply harmful way.

Manipulators know what to say to fulfil your basic social needs to be right or to be liked but use that information to bring you into harm's way. The more skilled the manipulator, the more powerful their influence. Skilled manipulators can force others to comply with their wishes, but truly masterful manipulators are ones that can achieve internalisation of their toxic worldview. On a small-scale, it's this kind of person that convinces their abused partner to stay with them. On a large-scale, it's this kind of person that convinces a nation that inhumane practices like slavery or torture are acceptable.

Contemporary psychologist George Simon names three basic qualities that separate a manipulator from a persuader. The first is the concealment of aggression (Simon, 2010). A manipulator is someone who secretly wishes another person harm. But rather than outright attacking their target, a manipulator will make the target feel comfortable, respected, liked, or otherwise socially influence the target to do as they wish before making their first aggressive move. Someone who is merely using the art of persuasion conceals no such harmful intentions (Simon, 2010).

The second quality of a manipulator is inventorying their target's vulnerabilities (Simon, 2010). All social influence, to some extent, is most potent when it appeals to someone's vulnerability. But manipulators specifically use things like fears, insecurities, and even past trauma to exert their influence over others. A negotiator has many tools in their toolbox. They can persuade others to do as they wish by appealing to weaknesses, but they can also appeal to strengths. Manipulators, on the other hand, specifically work from the places where their target is emotionally or psychologically weak, and often actively works to increase that weakness to increase their power over the target (Simon, 2010).

The third quality of the manipulator is what Simon calls 'ruthlessness' or a lack of remorse about what happens to the victim (Simon, 2010). Sometimes we persuade people to do things mistakenly. Perhaps you persuade your partner to take a promotion at work against their better judgment, only to find, to your chagrin, that they are miserable in her new position. Your chagrin is what makes you a persuader, not a manipulator. You may have used your powers of social influence to convince your partner to do something they didn't want to do, but you did so believing that their life would be improved if they followed your wishes. Real manipulators, on the other hand, never feel bad if their tactics put their targets in harm's way. Most manipulators are applying their skills intending to cause harm (Simon, 2010).

So, is everyone manipulative? No. But everyone does use social influence. Most people, however, do it without thinking. They influence and are influenced blindly, without ever truly understanding the psychology behind their communications or their behaviours. To be a good persuader, and to defend yourself against good manipulators, is to become aware of the rules of social influence. Rather than following your brain's natural communicative instincts, you'll learn to take a peek behind the proverbial curtain. Persuaders are intentional about how they choose to use their influence and are therefore much better able to spy when someone else is exerting influence over them.

2

RIGHT OR WRONG – THE ETHICS OF MANIPULATION

When Kelman first began publishing his theories of social influence in the 1950s, they made a lot of people uncomfortable. Many of our actions, he suggested, are not entirely within our control. Instead, much of our beliefs, attitudes, behaviours, and choices are in direct response to some kind of social influence, whether that's coming from another person, an advertisement, an official organisation such as a government, school, or church. And the people around us, in every interaction, are responding to the social influence that we exert upon them (Kelman, 1958). Is there free will at all? Or are all of our behaviours and attitudes merely the result of random patterns of social influence?

Though people continue to argue on this point, Kelman's theories completely changed the discipline of social psychology (Aronson, Wilson, Alert, & Sommers, 2015). His three levels of influence, compliance, identification, and internalisation, have been expanded in the field and today is commonly referred to only as 'conformity.' This is what happens when we change our beliefs, behaviours, and even our thoughts to be socially accepted by a group or community. It's by far the most pervasive form of manipulation (Aronson, Wilson, Alert, & Sommers, 2015). Every human, no matter how strong-willed, have adjusted their behaviours or attitudes at one point or another to maintain positive relationships with a particular social group (Aronson, Wilson, Alert, & Sommers, 2015). We make changes to please our families, friends, and co-workers. We make changes for romantic partners and changes for professional reasons.

In a classic psychology experiment of conformity, researchers put single test subjects in a room with seven other actors (unbeknownst to the subject, of course). They were shown tasks where they had to make easy judgement calls, such as, which was the longest or thinnest line amongst several options. After a few rounds of having the same answers as the rest, the actors ganged up and picked obviously *incorrect* answers. Since everyone announced their answers one after another before it came around to the subject, it was clear that he or she was the only one in the group that had a different answer. Across several experiments, Asch found that 75% of subjects conformed to the group's answer at least once, as compared to 1% who answered incorrectly when they were alone, and without peer pressure (Asch, 1951).

In many cases, we make the change knowingly, under-standing that we are modifying ourselves for the sake of the group. Although very normal and natural, it can become dangerous when the group begins asking us for things that we don't want to do, something that might make us feel uncomfortable or put us in danger. And someone who understands this innate, biological need within all humans for social acceptance could poten-tially use that understanding to harm others. "If you do this, you'll be one of us," is a message that we get all the time from people seeking to manipulate our behaviours to their purposes (Aronson, Wilson, Alert, & Sommers, 2015).

Conformity typically happens on a large scale (Aron-son, Wilson, Alert, & Sommers, 2015). Rather than bowing to the whims of one person, we make conscious or unconscious choices to help us better fit into a group. Because of this, we rarely consider the pressure to conform to be a form of 'manipulation.' But conformity isn't always an accident of group dynamics. Churches, cults, political parties, and other institutions that draw clear lines between members and outsiders provide their members with strict, clear guidelines of behaviour and attitude. These behaviours and attitudes separate members from outsiders. Deviating from the accepted rules of conduct marks you as an outsider. To be entirely acceptable to the group, you must fully conform (Aronson, Wilson, Alert, & Sommers, 2015). Is this conformity? Or is it something more sinister?

Advertisements and companies also use the psychology of conformity to their ends. Many advertisements seek to play to widespread insecurities or magnify perceived weaknesses in the viewer. The solution to their feelings of insecurity or not-belonging, inevitably, is whatever product or service the advertisement is promoting. 'Branding' takes this concept a step further, creating pseudo-communities and identities around their products. If you are a paying customer, a brand suggests, then that makes you a certain kind of person. Buying our products or participating in our services is a marker that you belong to a particular type of community or social grouping (Aronson, Wilson, Alert, & Sommers, 2015).

Micro-aggressive behaviours toward minority populations is another form of conformity that can hardly be seen as accidental (Aronson, Wilson, Alert, & Sommers, 2015). Instead of overt acts of racism, hate, or violence, micro-aggressions are subtle and challenging for the target to describe, especially to people who are not in the minority demographic. Companies that list "ethnic hairstyles" as being against their dress code is an all too common form of micro-aggression. Industries that ask men to shave their beards or women to cover their shoulders are also micro-aggressions. TV stations refusing to air shows that feature same-sex couples, but listing other reasons for their refusal, is a micro-aggression. These and a thousand other phrases, social norms, and group policies are subtle ways to control the attitudes and behaviours of minority populations, intending to make them more like the majority population. To be safe and accepted by the society they live in, people in minority populations find themselves always having to modify behaviours or attitudes that identify them as a minority. This is conformity, but it's a type of compliance that many groups choose to continue applying even after they've been made aware of the psychological pressures their rules or policies cause. If the group were a person, we would consider this manipulation (Aronson, Wilson, Alert, & Sommers, 2015).

However, many scientists, thinkers, and businesspeople have made the argument that the rules of conformity, social influence, and persuasion are beneficial to society (Aronson, Wilson, Alert, & Sommers, 2015). If compliance is used to promote LGBTQIIA+ rights or reducing pollution, then isn't that a good thing? Law enforcement, especially in recent years, has used the study of persuasion to transform the way that they interrogate prisoners, negotiate for hostages, and profile serial killers. Persuasion tactics have been successfully used by spies, journalists, and government agencies to profile and catch mass shooters, rehabilitate members of terrorist groups, and combat the persuasive tactics used by hate groups to recruit new members. So, is it right or wrong? Is using social influence merely an advanced form of the communication tactics we all employ naturally? Or does the intent to influence, by definition, constitute manipulation? Are the same tactics 'good' and 'bad' depending on the intention? Or are we all Machiavellians, believing that the end justifies the means?

THE PROSECUTION

When used in a harmful or abusive way, especially by an individual, social influence is typically referred to as 'manipulation.' The reasons that manipulation is unethical as a practice are relatively obvious. Using a person's psychology as a weapon against them is still a form of attack and abuse. Doing anything with the intentional attempt to harm must undoubtedly be considered unethical.

But many practices that call themselves 'persuasion' or 'conformity' could be called manipulation if looked at from a different angle. For example, manipulation is often defined as attempting to change someone's behaviour for the sake of personal gain. But aren't advertisements and business negotiations seeking to do just that? Is it unethical for stores to place products in ways that make customers more likely to buy them, or is that only good business practice? And these questions become even murkier in interpersonal relationships. If you're using persuasive tactics to convince your partner to let you turn the spare bedroom into a personal study, isn't this manipulation? You certainly benefit from the study, but does anyone else? Is it even wrong to want something for yourself?

To help answer these questions, social scientists and cognitive theorists have proposed several tests for businesses and other organisations to determine whether they are using forms of 'ethical' persuasion (Ethics of Persuasion: Public Speaking/Speech Communication, n.d.). The TARES test is a series of questions that can be applied to speeches and presentations. For an address to be both persuasive and ethical, according to the test, it must convey five distinct aspects: the truthfulness of the message, the authenticity of the persuader, respect for the audience, and equality of the persuasive appeal (Ethics of Persuasion: Public Speaking/Speech Communication, n.d.).

This sounds wonderful in theory and seems to set specific guidelines for political and official persuasion. If you represent your message truthfully and authentically, then it's not wrong to use a little extra persuasion to get that message across, right? The trouble with this test, however, is that many of Hitler's speeches would pass it with flying colours. Hitler believed what he was saying and made his intentions very clear in his famous speeches. But rather than being horrified, people loved him. Why? Persuasion. Hitler was a master persuader, and so he managed to convince an entire nation to believe some pretty horrible things. Things that he believed. Truthfully and authentically conveying an unethical message, many would argue, is still wrong.

Fitzpatrick and Gautier have developed a series of questions for businesspeople to evaluate the ethical veracity of their pitches (Ethics of Persuasion: Public Speaking/Speech Communication, n.d.). These questions are as follows:

- For what purpose is persuasion being employed?
- Toward what choices and with what consequences for individual lives is persuasion being used?
- Does the persuasion, in this case, contribute to or interfere with the decision-making process for its target audience?

Though these questions have been made for business pitches, they could be applied to any persuasive situation. The purpose of employing social influence does ultimately seem to be the deciding factor when it comes to determining the ethics of its usage (Ethics of Persuasion: Public Speaking/Speech Communication, n.d.). If the purpose is to control or do harm to another person, then it's most certainly manipulation and is therefore unethical. If its purpose is to help another person, on the other hand, then we could consider it ethical, an alternative strategy to outright fighting or giving directions. And if the purpose is for personal gain, then Fitzpatrick and Gautier direct us to the second question. What consequences does your strong influence have for the other person? If the other person loses nothing by giving you what you want, then it can still be considered ethical by this metric. If they do stand to lose something, then employing social influence would be regarded as manipulation (Ethics of Persuasion: Public Speaking/Speech Communication, n.d.).

It's only the last question that addresses the issue of 'truth' or 'honesty.' Employing specific tactics like 'mirroring' – deliberately imitating the postures and gestures of the person opposite you to establish rapport – presents you in a certain way and convinces the other person to feel relaxed and trusting around you. But if you give them the truth while they are in that state, then you cannot be said to have misled them. If, on the other hand, you are telling lies or omitting information that you know is critical to the other person's decision-making process, you are no longer persuading but manipulating. And, perhaps most importantly of all, if you present yourself as trustworthy, but your ultimate intention is to harm the other person. Even adjusting your body language to seem 'friendly' must be considered a lie (Ethics of Persuasion: Public Speaking/Speech Communication, n.d.).

Ironically, using this metric makes things a bit clearer from an interpersonal perspective. If you intend to help (or at least, not to harm) another person, then employing persuasion tactics to influence their decision cannot be considered manipulation. But this still leaves us to wonder about large-scale social influencers like marketers and government officials. For what purpose is persuasion being used is a fundamental question. In the case of advertisements, the aim is almost always making money and inspiring customer loyalty. In the case of governing bodies, the purpose is almost always to gain more votes, possibly make money, and inspire constituent loyalty. Are these purposes 'ethical' or 'unethical'? Without a doubt, persuasion is almost always employed in professional and official settings for personal gain. The most important question, then, seems to be the second. What are the consequences for individual lives as a direct result of the influence being employed? Who, if anyone, stands to be harmed by using persuasive tactics? And does the influencer care if that harm is done?

THE DEFENCE

The difference between persuasion and manipulation, at its core, is intention. But that intention can have a significant impact on the methods one chooses to employ when deciding to influence another person. Ultimately, persuasion involves presenting information to another person in a way that will help them to make an informed decision. The way that you present that information can have a significant influence on how the other person makes the decision. But, when persuading, you always understand and respect that the choice is ultimately not yours to make. Persuading is not about tricking or forcing, it's about well, influencing. It's subtle, but it's not underhanded. It's roundabout, but it's not trickery. When persuading, there's no need to spin facts, omit information, or rely on personal biases to make your point. Persuasion, more often than not, is about mannerisms. The way that you present yourself and your case is what influences the other person, not your case itself (Cialdini, 1984).

Manipulation, on the other hand, is inherently deceptive. Even if every single thing you say is right, if you present yourself as trustworthy when you intend to harm, then you're deceiving the other person. Using persuasive tactics to justify actions or beliefs that cause harm to others is also manipulation. Rather than taking responsibility for your actions or presenting your reasons for behaving the way that you did, you are trying to change the other person's attitudes to absolve yourself of social responsibility.

Persuasion often works hand-in-hand with honesty and integrity (Cialdini, 1984). If you go into a negotiation believing that the deal will be beneficial with both parties, then there's no need for deception. Making the other person comfortable around you is merely being polite. The ethical applications for persuasive tactics become more evident the further you move from business and political settings, as well. Using persuasion to convince a violent criminal to release his hostages is hardly unethical. They are using persuasion tactics in interrogations if vastly preferable to torture, which could be considered manipulation unto itself. Much is made of the "psychological games" that FBI and CIA agents use to 'trick' people into confessions. But if the other person is indeed guilty, then persuading them to admit that guilt is hardly unethical. Again, respect for the other person's freedom of choice is critical. Manipulation would be influencing someone to confess that you knew or even suspected was innocent. Making an innocent person believe they are guilty of something is mind control, a very advanced and insidious form of manipulation. But removing the psychological barriers, someone has erected to hide the truth of their actions? If lying is an essential piece of why manipulation itself is unethical, then persuading someone, to tell the truth, can hardly be considered an unethical practice (Cialdini, 1984).

Ultimately, the end doesn't justify the means (Williams, 2011). Torturing a criminal for a confession is still unethical. At that point, you are convincing them to tell the truth, and you're applying force and intentionally harming someone to force them to do what you want. Or consider the 2002 invasion of Iraq on the part of the United States. This war was justified based on large-scale manipulation. Tales of stockpiled weapons and vague implications of Saddam Hussein's involvement in the 9/11 attacks are the tactics that ultimately convinced people all over the world that the invasion was justified. The goal of removing a tyrant, on the other hand, would seem to be a noble cause, and no one would argue with Saddam Hussein's human rights records. Had facts been used to persuade people and governments that the war was justified, presenting both the merits and risks of the invasion in an honest way, the invasion may have been viewed in a very different light. But the manipulation and the resulting exposure of that manipulation automatically negated whatever just cause the US government may have had, and the resulting division and scepticism have caused far more harm than good. Intent to remove a tyrant is not enough to justify using manipulation to gain support for the cause. The methods of influence, the warping of information, and the intent to deceive or harm all contribute to distinguishing between the ethical practice of persuasion and the unethical practice of manipulation (Williams, 2011).

This same logic applies to interpersonal relationships. We rarely label people who are charming and persuasive as 'manipulative.' It's when we get a sense that something is not quite right, that the person's true intentions don't seem to match their mannerisms, that we begin to think of someone as manipulative. If someone convinces you to do something good for you, then that feels good. We often label that as 'empowering' or 'supporting' someone. They may be using tactics to make you feel more comfortable or using persuasive language to convince you to listen to them, but their intentions are never hidden. Persuasion, ultimately, is the art of saying something to someone in the way they are most likely to hear it (Cialdini, 1984). Manipulation, on the other hand, necessitates that something is being hidden. Manipulators convince you to do things that you genuinely don't want to do or things that put you in harm's way. They employ manipulation, however, to convince you that it's something that might be good for you. Foisting the choice onto you absolves them of any social responsibility. It's still an attack, and it's still caused harm, it's just more subtle than making threats or using force.

3

DARK PSYCHOLOGY 101

Psychology recognises three personality traits that make someone far more likely to use social influence in a manipulative way. These personality types, referred to as the "dark triad," are Machiavellianism, narcissism, and psychopathy (Paulhus & Williams, 2002). Understanding and recognising these personality types form the backbone of a pseudo-scientific study called dark psychology.

Though dark psychology as a discipline is considered a pseudoscience, its concepts are all based on accepted scientific research. Research on the dark triad is used across the fields of applied psychology, especially in law enforcement, clinical psychology, and even business management (Paulhus & Williams, 2002). People that score high on these traits aren't just more likely to be manipulative, they're also more likely to commit crimes, create problems for the organisations and communities they belong to, and generally cause social distress (Kaufman, Yaden, Hyde, & Tsukayama, 2019). On an interpersonal level, those who present strongly with traits from the dark triad tend to be less compassionate than others, as well as less agreeable, empathetic, satisfied with their lives, and less likely to believe that they and/or others are good (Kaufman, Yaden, Hyde, & Tsukayama, 2019).

The three personality components of the dark triad are considered distinct from one another. You can be narcissistic without being psychopathic or have strong Machiavellian traits without being a narcissist. However, even the strong presence of just one of these traits is enough to assume that person is going to have a manipulative personal style (Horowitz & Strack, 2010). And unfortunately, the presence of one of these traits makes it that much more likely that the other two traits also form a strong basis of your personality.

All three of the dark triad's personality traits are characterised by a manipulative interpersonal style (Horowitz & Strack, 2010). But they also have distinct components that separate them from the other two, as well as separating them from other personality traits. These three traits are fundamental to watch for in other people. Dark psychology, as a discipline, is devoted to recognising these traits in others before they have a chance to start working their manipulative influence and counter their manipulations with defensive psychological strategies.

The discovery of the dark triad began in the 1980s, with the development of a personality-assessment model called the OCEAN model—this model rates individuals based on the presence of five distinct traits. Different combinations of traits form a distinct personality type (Rothmann & Coetzer, 2003).

The five traits that the OCEAN model looks for are openness to experience, conscientiousness, extraversion, agreeableness, and neuroticism (Rothmann & Coetzer, 2003). Within each category contains two distinct personality types, depending on how you score. Within openness to experience, you are either inventive/curious or consistent/cautious. The conscientiousness separates those who are efficient/organised from those who are extravagant/careless. Extraversion determines whether you are outgoing/energetic or solitary/reserved. Agreeableness distinguishes between those who are friendly/compassionate and challenging/callous. Finally, neuroticism determines whether you are sensitive/nervous or resilient/confident (Rothmann & Coetzer, 2003).

As you can see, none of these personality traits is inherently negative or positive. The assessment was initially designed to determine how different personality traits tend to interact in professional (especially business) settings. But further personality research has found links between the dark triad and specific aspects of the OCEAN model. Those who score as challenging/callous, extravagant/careless, and sensitive/nervous altogether be far more likely to present with dark personality traits (Jakobwitz & Egan, 2006). Challenging/callous, especially, seems to be an indicator of dark triad personalities (Klimstra, Jeronimus, Sijsema, & Denissen, 2020). It seems that it's almost impossible to be both friendly/compassionate and manipulative at the same time.

WELCOME TO THE DARK SIDE

The problem is that those with dark triad personalities almost always *appear* to be friendly and compassionate on the surface. Someone that you might say is exceptionally agreeable may be callous beneath the surface. This is the root of their manipulation. It's what makes dark personalities so challenging to spot and defend against. It's how they climb quickly and easily into positions of power, where they become that much harder to surrender even when their real personalities have been revealed. And it's what makes them very difficult to study or categorise from a scientific perspective (Simon, 2010).

Dark psychology focuses exclusively on dark triad traits for this reason, with the intent of learning as much as we can about how these traits manifest in individuals, and how to combat their psychological games most efficiently. While people can and do present with a combination of dark triad traits, some traits are more likely to appear together than others. Each trait seems to be more closely related to one of the other two. And all of the dark triad personalities tend to present with distinctive scoring patterns on the OCEAN assessment.

Machiavellianism

Machiavellianism is characterised by frequent exploitation of others, a noticeable absence of morality, unemotional callousness, and a toxically high level of self-interest (Jakobwitz & Egan, 2006). Machiavellians are perhaps the most manipulative of all, as they are consistently and intentionally stepping on others to promote themselves. Machiavellians don't care who they have to hurt to get what they want. They are ruthlessly ambitious, with no moral qualms about destroying the lives of others to benefit from that destruction.

They can be recognised by their cynicism (Furnham, Richards, & Paulhus, 2013). They are not cynical in a doubtful or sceptical sense, however. They are cynical in an amoral sense. Machiavellians are utterly unprincipled, believing that the end justifies the means, but they have a way of rationalising their unethical behaviours to make them more acceptable to others. No matter what manipulative tactics they may employ, Machiavellians also tend to come across as cold. It's challenging for them to simulate warmth or compassion. They believe that manipulation is not only entirely justified, but that it's the key to success in life. These are the kinds of people who will argue that it's 'necessary' to do hurtful and damaging things to get what you need out of life (Furnham, Richards, & Paulhus, 2013). Beware anyone who seems a little too comfortable with making hard decisions that may hurt others.

Machiavellians almost always score as challenging/callous and extravagant/careless, regardless of how they score in other areas (Paulhus & Williams, 2002). They also seem to be very intensely correlated with psychopathy. Those who present with strong Machiavellian traits are far more likely to be psychopaths than narcissists (Vernon, Villani, Vickers, & Harris, 2008).

Narcissism

Narcissism is characterised by grandiosity, pride, egotism, and a noticeable lack of empathy (Kohut, 2014). Narcissists tend to be dramatic, making every single social situation about them. This doesn't always take the form of dramatic displays, but it does take the form of dramatic emotions within the other person. They have a way of making you feel wracked with guilt over the smallest mistakes, or making you feel like anything wrong that happens in their life is somehow your fault. They have a tangible sense of entitlement. Though they often play the victim to win sympathy and concern from others, the underlying message is that they were *owed* your affection. They have no problem demanding excesses of time, energy, and even money from the people around them, subtly or overtly punishing those who dare to act in a way that doesn't directly serve their interests. Even when they're playing hurt, they are ultimately the dominant partner, behaving with a sense of superiority over others (Cory, Merritt, Mrug, & Pamp, 2008). Their concerns are the ultimate concerns, and they expect everyone around them to be, do, and say as they command.

However, narcissists aren't looking for attention—they're looking for control. Making everything about them is far more subtle than it sounds. They have a way of making *you* believe that everything is about them, too, which can cause you a significant amount of emotional and social stress as you find yourself going further and further out of your way to make them happy.

Narcissists almost always score as outgoing/energetic, inventive/curious, and challenging/callous, regardless of how they score in other areas (Paulhus & Williams, 2002). Narcissists are also strongly correlated with psychopathy. Narcissists are far more likely to be psychopaths than they are to be Machiavellians (Vernon, Villani, Vickers, & Harris, 2008).

Psychopathy

Psychopathy is characterised by extreme antisocial behaviours, impulsivity, selfishness, callous and unemotional traits, and remorselessness (Frick & White, 2008). 'Antisocial' is a word often misused to mean shy, sullen, or withdrawn in social situations. But in the world of psychology, antisocial means behaving in ways that intentionally cause harm to other people (Frick & White, 2008). Stealing for fun is an example of antisocial behaviour, as is spiteful vandalism, sexually humiliating another person, or purposely smoking around someone you know is sensitive to the smoke. Psychopaths almost seem to enjoy making others feel angry, uncomfortable, or unsafe (Frick & White, 2008).

Psychopaths are often considered the 'darkest' of the dark triad because they are the most likely to do direct physical harm to other people (Rauthmann, 2011). Their complete lack of empathy can be recognisable in them. Unlike Machiavellians, who believe that their manipulation is necessary for them to succeed in life, psychopaths simply don't care who they hurt, and even seek to hurt people just for the fun of it. In this way, they are also characterised by a penchant for impulsivity and thrill-seeking (Rauthmann, 2011).

Psychopaths have the most distinctive presentation in the OCEAN assessment. A combination of outgoing/energetic, challenging/callous, extravagant/careless, sensitive/nervous, and inventive/curious is almost a guaranteed indicator of psychopathy (Vernon, Villani, Vickers, & Harris, 2008). Psychopathy is also the most common trait in the dark triad, equally as likely to present with narcissism or with Machiavellianism (Vernon, Villani, Vickers, & Harris, 2008).

In some people, dark triad traits can appear together, producing some particularly dangerous individuals. Someone can be a narcissistic psychopath, for example. But more often, while these traits may overlap, there's one personality trait that emerges more substantial than the other two. Becoming familiar with the dark triad can help you to recognise these patterns in other people. Merely recognising that someone you know has narcissistic or Machiavellian tendencies is a huge step toward becoming resistant to their manipulations. Manipulative interpersonal dealings characterise all three of the dark triad personalities, and this is what makes them truly dangerous. It's impossible to fully trust a psychopath or a narcissist because you can never trust that they have your best interests at heart. These personality types never persuade; they always manipulate. Their primary interests are their own, and their lack of empathy or compassion makes it nearly impossible for them to use social influence in a cooperative spirit (Paulhus & Williams, 2002).

THE DEVIL YOU KNOW

Researchers believe that a combination of biological and environmental factors contribute to the presence of a dark personality type. All three of the dark triad personality traits have been linked to distinct genetic patterns, arguably making the presence of these traits the sign of a disorder, something that is inherited rather than learned (Petrides, Vernon, Schermer, & Veselka, 2011). However, research has found narcissism and psychopathy to be much more inheritable than Machiavellianism (Furnham, Richards, & Paulhus, 2013).

On that same note, it seems that Machiavellianism, of the three traits, is the one most profoundly influenced by environmental factors (Vernon, Martin, Schermer, & Mackie, 2008). It seems that specific life situations, especially in early childhood, can cause someone to develop a Machiavellian personality later in life (Vernon, Martin, Schermer, & Mackie, 2008). All three dark triad traits, however, are triggered by unique life events and experiences. Someone can inherit the genetic patterns correlated with a dark personality type without ever developing or expressing those traits in their adult life. In other words, the genes that make up dark personality types have to be triggered early in life for someone to develop a fully formed dark personality (Vernon, Martin, Schermer, & Mackie, 2008).

Because of its genetic component, two of the dark triad types—narcissism and psychopathy—are considered pathological, something that must be treated and managed by a professional. However, for that to happen, the person in question has to recognise that they have a problem. Their dark personality traits have to cause these people to distress in their personal or professional lives before they seek professional help. Unfortunately, dark personalities very rarely cause the people they belong to any distress at all.

Studies have demonstrated that dark triad personality types are highly likely to be aggressive and racist (Jones & Paulhus, 2010). These personality types are far more likely to bully and abuse other people and are more likely to commit acts of violence motivated by racism or other forms of hate (Jones & Paulhus, 2010). Yet, studies have also shown that dark triad types are more likely to acquire leadership positions in the workplace than other kinds of people (Furnham, Richards, & Paulhus, 2013). Several studies have shown that dark personalities are quite commonly found at the upper-management and CEO level of business (Amernic & Craig, 2010). Not only have their personality traits not caused them any distress, but they've brought these people a great deal of wealth, success, and respect!

The reason for this, ultimately, is their penchant for manipulation. All people can manipulate, but dark triad types are the best and arguably the most dangerous because of their lack of empathy. The thing that stops many of us from taking our manipulations too far is a general sense of compassion and consideration for the feelings of others. Without a sense of compassion to temper them, however, dark triad personalities will use their skills to abuse, control, and subjugate other people until forced to stop. Often, that force comes in the form of law enforcement, as these personality types are highly likely to commit crimes (Amernic & Craig, 2010).

Manipulation gives dark triad types a great deal of power and control over others. Unfortunately, many of the traits that make them recognisable as dark personalities are also traits that society at large has come to respect and reward. Machiavellians, for example, are often praised for their ambition and are equally likely to be CEOs of major corporations as they are to be criminals (Amernic & Craig, 2010). Their innate ability to use social influence for personal gain often brings them a great deal of success and respect before someone is finally able to unmask them. Many dark triad personality types are never 'caught' by society at large. Individual people may learn to avoid them, but they simply move on to the next target.

One recent study found that people with dark triad personality traits are more likely to be judged as good-looking by strangers (Carter, Campbell, & Muncer, 2013). Upon closer examination, however, it turned out that this had nothing to do with the dark personality's physical features. Instead, it was found that all three dark personality types tend to spend a great deal of time on their looks (Carter, Campbell, & Muncer, 2013). Narcissists, especially, tend to be judged as physically attractive by others. One study of manipulation in the workplace found that physical appearance was the primary tool used by narcissists to get what they wanted from bosses, co-workers, and even clients (Jonason, Slomski, & Partyka, 2012). Machiavellians were found to be excessively charming in the workplace, while the primary manipulative weapon of psychopaths was found to be making threats (Jonason, Slomski, & Partyka, 2012).

Dark personality types don't look like ordinary people—they often look *better* than normal people. Even professional psychologists have found themselves taken in by the manipulations of dark personalities, not realising what was happening until it was too late. It's nearly impossible to spot a dark personality on the surface. The most effective way to both recognise and protect yourself against them is to recognise their manipulative strategies, and employ methods to defend against them.

Dark personalities are so good at what they do that an entire discipline of interpersonal studies has been developed around studying them. Dark psychology refers to the discipline of studying the methods dark triad personalities use to manipulate their targets, but it can also refer to the methods themselves. Dark psychology is social influence at its worst. It's what happens when people use our brain's natural social mechanisms to harm and control others. While anyone can be manipulative, many people can also learn to recognise and change their behaviour. A relationship with a manipulative person can be complicated. Still, there's hope for it to become healthy, especially if you learn some persuasive techniques of your own to even the playing field. But dark psychology should always be considered an attack. Dark personalities cannot change without a high level of intervention from a trained professional. If you find yourself the victim of dark psychology, the only appropriate response is to deploy your psycho-social defences and get as far away from that person as you possibly can.

4

MIND CONTROL AND
BRAINWASHING

Mind control and brainwashing are two of the most insidious forms of manipulation. Other names for these techniques include thought reform, psychological persuasion, coercive persuasion, thought control, and mental control. Regardless of what they're called, these two techniques are employed over time to change another person's perception, cognition, emotion, decision-making ability and behaviours, to the extent that the target has lost the freedom to make their own choices (Brainwashing techniques vs mind control, n.d.). The term 'brainwashing' was coined by Edward Hunter, a researcher in the 1950s working with American soldiers who had been imprisoned by the Chinese, and it wasn't until the late 1990s that it was distinguished from mind control (Brainwashing techniques vs mind control, n.d.). However, while the words may be new, the tactics are ancient and have been successfully used by both individuals and organisations for thousands of years. While it's relatively easy to see brainwashing or mind control happening to someone else, it's nearly impossible to recognise when it's happening to you.

Though the two terms are often used interchangeably, they differ slightly in approach. Both manipulative forms employ several different techniques to strip their targets of their ability to think or make decisions for themselves. There is no one set method of mind control or brainwashing, and the same manipulator will often employ various techniques to achieve the same goal. Brainwashing and mind control are both ongoing processes–they don't happen overnight. This is one of the primary reasons why these techniques are so difficult to recognise until it's too late. The changes to the target's behaviours, beliefs, and attitudes happen very slowly, and over a long time (Brainwashing vs mind control, n.d.). Perhaps the most alarming feature of mind control and brainwashing is that awareness of the process is not enough to protect you from it. Manipulators practising mind control and brainwashing can continue to influence their target even after the target has become aware that they're being manipulated. These techniques are employed with the intent to internalise, but they are still useful in compelling compliance in the target (Brainwashing vs mind control, n.d.).

Steve Hassan, a psychologist who spent over 30 years studying and treating ex-cult members, was the first to distinguish mind control and brainwashing as two different processes (Brainwashing vs mind control, n.d.). Brainwashing, according to his definition, happens when the manipulator has a hostile or overtly authoritative relationship to the target (Brainwashing vs mind control, n.d.). Prisons, schools, and the military are all ideal places for a person or organisation to practice brainwashing. Often, the target sees the manipulator as an enemy at the beginning of the process, or at the very least as an authoritarian figure. Brainwashing begins by inducing compliance in the target. They know that to survive or escape physical harm, they must do as the manipulator wishes (Brainwashing vs mind control, n.d.).

Physical torture and abuse are standard tools used by brainwashers (Brainwashing vs mind control, n.d.). Often, the point of this is to compel the target to lie about their attitudes or beliefs, saying what the manipulator wants to hear simply to escape punishment. Slowly but surely, however, the target is forced to repeat the lies so many times that they begin to believe them. What began as compliance becomes internalisation until the target can no longer distinguish between their attitudes and beliefs and the ones that have been forced on them by the brainwasher. Even after the manipulator has released control over the target, the target may still find it challenging to return to their original thoughts or opinions without a great deal of help from others (Brainwashing vs mind control, n.d.).

Mind control, on the other hand, happens when the manipulator is considered by the target to be a friend or a helper (Brainwashing vs mind control, n.d.). In the case of mind control, the target rarely knows that they are being manipulated. Instead, they believe that their relationship with the manipulator is genuine and believe that changes in their behaviour or attitudes are ones that the target made themself. If the manipulator makes overt suggestions or requests, the target is happy to comply, believing that the manipulator is just giving them friendly advice or guidance and overestimating their ability to refuse (Brainwashing vs mind control, n.d.).

Mind control is prevalent in cults, marriages, and workplaces. Cult members never believe that they're being controlled or manipulated. Even when disillusioned, they often continue to believe that their thoughts and actions were their own while they were involved with the cult. Victims of mind control always believe that they are making their own decisions, and it can be challenging to convince them otherwise (Brainwashing vs mind control, n.d.).

This distinction is incredibly important when it comes to defending against or recovering from these techniques. While a brainwashing victim knows that harm was done to them, it can be complicated for someone who has been subjected to mind control to understand that the manipulator was acting with ill-intent. Mind control victims often believe that they simply made bad decisions or that they were unaware of the true nature of the manipulator (Brainwashing vs mind control, n.d.). They don't realise that the manipulator was employing psychological tactics to control their behaviour actively. The manipulator wasn't just charming or attractive–they were intentionally seeking to cause their target harm. This is why many cult members, even after becoming disillusioned with the cult, will still consider the group leader to be a kind and helpful person. In personal or romantic relationships, if the target does manage to leave the manipulator, they often continue to believe that the problems in the relationship were their fault (Brainwashing vs mind control, n.d.).

BRAINWASHING – USAGE AND DEFENCE

Unfortunately, the only way to defend oneself against brainwashing is to escape from the brainwasher. Robert Lifton is a researcher working with American prisoners of war. After years of studying and rehabilitating its victims, he has outlined brainwashing as a 12-step process (Brainwashing vs mind control, n.d.).

Step 1: Assault on Identity

The first step in the brainwashing process is to challenge the target at the level of their identity. Prisoners of war are often physically abused and tortured while everything they say is contradicted. The combination of physical pain and emotional distress causes the target to begin to doubt themselves.

This may be much less obvious or dramatic in a relationship – the manipulator could hide behind "jokes" that humiliate their target with constant criticism and unrealistic expectations, causing the person being manipulated to doubt their self-worth. They may come across as trying to help by pointing out everything that they do wrong. Ironically, crippling someone's self-esteem paves the way for the target to lean on the manipulator as a crutch for praise and reinforcement.

Step 2: Establishment of Guilt

Lifton's prisoners and other victims of brainwashing report feeling burdened with a tremendous sense of guilt. Ultimately, this causes the target to believe that they deserve punishment. Even if the target maintains a hostile relationship with the manipulator, the manipulator is no longer seen as unjustified in inflicting pain or other punishment on the target. At this point, the target will begin to feel responsible for all of their faults, and for anything that goes wrong in either their own life or in the life of the manipulator. Making a mistake, doing something poorly, or even being part of a situation in which things don't go according to plan can make the target feel wracked with guilt and responsibility. These can all incur punishment on the part of the brainwasher, but as the target assumes more and more responsibility, they resist punishment less and less.

Step 3: Self-Betrayal

At this point, the target is typically asked by the manipulator to renounce the people who are closest to them. First, they are expected to renounce more superficial relationships like those with friends and colleagues, and they are expected to renounce their families and even their core beliefs. Any doubts or ambivalences they may have had to these people or institutions in the past are played up by the manipulator as evidence that the target's previous life was toxic. Eventually, this causes the target to psychologically divorce themselves from their past, effectively destroying their sense of self.

In relationships, manipulators accumulate their power and influence over their target by systematically trying to isolate them from their closest circle of friends and family who may recognise the toxic relationship and try to extract the target from it. This could be in the form of planting negative thoughts about certain friends to sow doubt in the target's relationship with them, or, bolder yet; they may even try to plant seeds of doubt about the target's character with their friends and family to get them to stay away. Targets who find themselves abandoned or doubtful of their relationships resolve to stay with the one person who seems to be steadfast – the manipulator.

Step 4: The Breaking Point

At this point, the target realises that there is no way to escape the horror and pain they are experiencing. They begin to consider the possibility of death seriously. In extreme cases, many people even hope for death. Delusions and even fear-induced hallucinations are common at this point. The target becomes desperate for a way to escape the pain and punishment inflicted on them by the manipulator.

This usually translates into a break-up or, in non-romantic relationships, a coldness or distancing that target builds between themselves and their manipulator. This could be when the target first realises that the problem may not lie in them. The target manages to establish some form of distance between themselves and their manipulator – however, this relief (for both the target and their close ones) could be short-lived.

Step 5: Leniency

Just when the target believes there is no hope left, the manipulator suddenly changes tactics. Rather than punishment and pain, the manipulator offers a friendly face or speaks to the target with a kind voice. The manipulator may break down and cry, offer romantic gifts. This sudden kindness and vulnerability always come simultaneously with an offer to renounce their old ways and embrace the new life. Blindsided by this show of kindness or remorse, it is easy for the target to believe in their manipulator's promise of change and gives in to their demands.

Step 6: Confession

To further humiliate and dehumanise the target, the manipulator often forces the target to confess to some sort of past wrongdoing openly. Often, these 'wrongdoings' are simply attitudes or behaviours that run contrary to what the manipulator wants from them. Failure to confess, or to confess with convincing sincerity, often results in punishment. To escape this, targets will often make up 'crimes,' merely saying what they think the manipulator wants to hear. Eventually, however, the target begins to believe their confessions, and by extension, believes that these things are crimes that they deserve to be punished.

Step 7: The Channelling of Guilt

At this point, the target's feelings of guilt deepen. Rather than feeling guilty about their actions or beliefs, the target begins to feel guilty about who they are. They believe that their entire existence is something shameful and abhorrent and that the only 'right' way to be is to be the way the manipulator wants them to be.

Step 8: Re-education

At this point, the target is motivated to change their behaviours and beliefs following the manipulator's wishes. To further repress their true identity, the manipulator will often magnify the target's actual weaknesses and correlate them with some aspect of their previous identity. For example, a bad habit or a lack of talent in some area might be linked with the target's family life, nationality, or education. To correct that flaw, the manipulator suggests, the target must embrace the new way of life offered by the manipulator.

Step 9: Progress and Harmony

The more the target changes to conform to the manipulator's wishes, the more the manipulator treats them like a human being again. Acceptable thoughts and behaviours are rewarded with praise, privileges, and respect, while unacceptable thoughts are punished. Escaping the horror of their torture is often enough to motivate the target to finally and fully embrace the new personality that's been forced on them by the manipulator.

Step 10: The Final Confession

While previous confessions were smaller or more private, the final confession is often treated with great formality. There may be witnesses or even some kind of ceremony for the target to publicly reject their own identity and verbalise that they have seen the error of their previous ways.

Step 11: Rebirth

At this point, the target is allowed to resume their 'normal' life, but their entire identity has been changed. Good behaviour continues to be rewarded, while bad behaviour continues to be punished. However, the nature of the punishment is typically less severe at this point, as the manipulator has entirely remade the target's identity. The threat of harm is no longer necessary to motivate the target to want to please the manipulator.

Step 12: Release

At this point, the manipulator lets go of their hold on the target, releasing the target back into the world. Having their new identity challenged by old friends and family members is often extremely traumatic from the target, who will often seek to be reunited with the manipulator or the group that the manipulator belonged.

MIND CONTROL – USAGE AND DEFENCE

In 1978, the charismatic cult-leader, Jim Jones, led the largest mass murder-suicide in history of 918 of his followers, who drank cyanide-laced *Flavor Aid* to their demise. He convinced parents to poison their children first to ensure they would not back out of their decision (Kennedy, 2018). Of the 918 dead, 304 were children. Before their deaths, the community of followers were living in squalid conditions with barely enough food. How Jim Jones had his entire congregation enthralled despite the ruthless suffering he put them through has been one of the most significant landmark cases on mind control.

Like brainwashing, the ultimate goal of mind control is to destroy the target's identity, replacing it with a pseudo-personality that holds the beliefs, values, and ideas of the manipulator. However, the techniques of mind control are often much more subtle than brainwashing. The manipulator often lures the target in by making them think that the manipulator is a friend or a guiding authority figure like a mentor, teacher, or healer (Brainwashing vs mind control, n.d.).

Mind control techniques are also almost always shame and guilt-based. The target is often told that they are weak or defective in some way, but that those weaknesses are not their fault. All of their weaknesses and flaws are linked to different facets of the target's life, such as the society they live in or the way their parents raised them. The more the target hears this, the more they start to question who they are (Brainwashing vs mind control, n.d.).

Fear is another powerful weapon of mind control. Often, the manipulator will paint a grim picture of what the target will eventually become if they continue to live as they are. Once the target starts to fear that future, the manipulator then offers alternative beliefs and behaviours to help them become a 'better' person.

Mind control plays to the emotions of the target, making them feel good about the changes they are making to themselves, often packaging conforming to the manipulator's wishes as an act of personal transformation, or even liberation. Making the target feel good about the changes also makes them less likely to think critically about what the manipulator is asking from them, and can even cause them to become defensive when other people point out the changes in a negative way (Brainwashing vs mind control, n.d.).

Mind control, like brainwashing, also involves a system of punishment-and-reward. However, the punishments inflicted by mind controllers are often much more subtle. Rather than beating and torturing the target, a mind controller may withhold affection or attention from the target if they behave in an 'unacceptable' way. The manipulator may also humiliate or criticise the target for any behaviour that isn't under the pseudo-personality the manipulator is trying to instil in them. Some mind controllers do become physically or sexually abusive, but this is often after an intimate relationship has already been established between the manipulator and the target (Brainwashing vs mind control, n.d.).

Hypnosis is a very advanced form of mind control, with a set of skills that take years of practice to learn and execute effectively. Double agendas are another common tactic employed by mind controllers, in which the target believes they are getting one thing, but in reality, they are getting something else. "Love bombing" is a technique that involves showering the target with love and affection, especially as a reward for good behaviour. Many mind controllers also encourage their victims to play childish games or behave childishly in some other way. This causes a feeling of age regression in the target that magnifies the manipulator's power of authority over them (Brainwashing vs mind control, n.d.).

In the case of cults and mind-controlling organisations, new members are rarely given any time to themselves. They are always accompanied by a senior member of the organisation to prevent them from getting enough time to think objectively about whether or not they genuinely want to stay. The financial commitment is also something that mind-controlling organisations use to encourage psychological commitment. If you're paying dues or membership fees, always make sure you know how those funds are being used (Brainwashing vs mind control, n.d.).

Mind controllers seem benevolent but be very careful of someone who never allows you to question or criticise them. No one likes to be challenged, and compliance with rules and policies are an integral part of every organisation. But even the most advanced companies and reputable universities allow their staff members to ask questions and make constructive criticisms. If no questions or criticisms are acceptable in any form, then you should get as far away from that person or institution as you can.

Unfortunately, mind control is all around us. Advertisements, casinos, and shopping malls are all designed to influence the way people think and behave. Companies are getting better at targeting audiences by digitally stalking them and mining their data to prey on their purchasing tendencies. Data has also been used to influence elections, encircling us into the groups that agree with us rather than letting us face off with people who have different views.

The most important weapon you have against it is your ability to think critically. When watching the news or reading articles online, always ask yourself if all sides of the story have been told. Make sure that you double-check facts and figures. Ask yourself if there may be other perspectives on the story before believing it completely.

Also, be aware of how you talk about yourself to other people. What is your identity? Who are you? When you meet someone at a party for the first time, how do you describe yourself? What details do you choose to share, and which do you choose to omit? If you find yourself repressing things that you once loved or sharing details that wouldn't usually be important to casual conversations, take a moment to ask yourself why that is. Is this a natural moment of growth and change for you? Or is there an influential person in your life that's been making subtle suggestions about how you could or should be acting?

We get feedback and suggestions from people all the time. Friends, family members, co-workers, and even strangers we meet at parties can all have suggestions for what we 'should' or 'shouldn't' do. But remember that real friends love you as you are, not as you could be. A true friend won't punish you for disagreeing with them or make you feel guilty for not doing something they asked you to do. If you find yourself wearing certain clothes, reading individual books, or making even more significant life decisions because a person might "get mad" if you don't, definitely take a moment to re-evaluate your relationship with that person.

5

NLP – THEORY, RESEARCH, AND DEVELOPMENT

NLP AS A SCIENCE

Neuro-Linguistic Programming, or NLP, was developed in the 1970s Richard Bandler and John Grinder (Bandler & Grinder, 1979). NLP is a pseudoscience that argues that language has a direct and measurable effect on the brain's neurological processes. The essence of the discipline is a series of targeted, language-based techniques that, if applied successfully, can alter the way you think by changing the neurological pathways in your brain.

Many people use NLP on themselves to achieve life goals, treat physical or mental illnesses, and even to overcome learning disorders. It is used variously as a self-help tool, a persuasive tactic, and a tool for manipulative influence. It all depends on who is using the technique and what their ultimate goals are (Dilts, 1980).

Bandler and Grinder claimed that they had discovered a methodology through which they could codify the structures inherent to any complex human activity, and then use that codification to model those structures and eventually learn the activity. The initial publication of their techniques was published in 1975 and titled *The Structure of Magic I: A Book about Language and Therapy.*

The technique they used to codify certain behaviours is called 'modelling.' Bandler and Grinder began using this technique on patients to form what they called a 'meta-model' of the client's behaviours (Bandler, Grinder, Satir, & Bateson, 2005). They would use this meta-model first to gather information about the client's subjective representational structures, and then use that information to challenge the client's language and eventually change their underlying thinking. They claimed that, by challenging what they called linguistic distortions, specifying generalisations, and recovering deleted information from the client's statements, they could then use the transformational grammatical concept of "surface structure" to gain a complete representation of the underlying "deep structure." Making changes to the deep structure is what ultimately leads to changes in behaviour (Bandler, Grinder, Satir, & Bateson, 2005).

This radical new approach to psychotherapy started to gain public notice at the end of the 1970s. The Esalen Institute in Big Sur, California, was a hub for the human potential movement that was sweeping across the United States at the time (Clancy & Yorkshire, 1989). Fuelled by the belief that human beings were capable of far more than modern science supposed, the institute hosted workshops and invited people from all over the country to speak about various kinds of therapies. Inspired by many of these sessions, Grinder and Bandler began to market their technique, insisting that it wasn't only limited to psychotherapy and that it could be used as a business tool as well (Clancy & Yorkshire, 1989). Finally, they hosted a ten-day instructional workshop on the technique in Santa Cruz, California, after which the method became a national phenomenon (Clancy & Yorkshire, 1989). Bandler and Grinder began publishing more books, and eventually, a small community of students and interested psychotherapists started to form around the technique. Its popularity and rapid growth led to a wide variety of techniques and approaches to the core philosophies of the practice. It's usage by people as popular as the self-help guru Tony Robbins furthered public attention to the method (Clancy & Yorkshire, 1989).

Several people in a variety of disciplines have claimed to use NLP successfully to achieve many different things. More and more businesses are teaching NLP techniques to executives to use them in negotiations (Bandler & Grinder, 1979).

It may not cause any physical changes to the brain's neurological pathways or 'programming,' but it does seem to cause changes in the way people think about specific behaviours. It has a symbolic efficiency, which may not be useful from a clinical perspective but is critical for manipulation or persuasion.

A symbol is a powerful, persuasive tool, one used by artists, priests, and even marketing agencies every day. Symbols are potent persuaders because they appeal to the emotions (Langford, 1999). They aren't based on logic, and so can't be examined or argued. The emotional response to a powerful symbol is visceral and often unconscious, making symbol an easy way for a manipulator or negotiator to remain in control of the target's emotional state. Controlling the target's emotions, of course, makes it much easier to influence their behaviour and even their thoughts (Langford, 1999).

Symbolic religious gestures and rituals are performed to create specific emotional associations in the minds of the participants (Langford, 1999). Catholic priests claim to transform bread and wine into the physical body and blood of Jesus Christ at the end of every mass. Practitioners may understand that there was no literal, scientific transformation that took place, but they consume the communion gifts with reverence and awe just the same. The priest doesn't have to physically transform the wine to influence the thinking and behaviours of the congregation. Symbolic transformation is enough (Langford, 1999).

NLP practitioners do something similar, but the symbols that they transform are personal symbols, unique to their target (Bandler & Grinder, 1979). There doesn't have to be a measurable, cognitive change in the target's physical brain for the technique to be successful. The shift in an emotional association is enough to influence the target's thinking and behaviours (Bandler & Grinder, 1979).

NLP is founded on three core psychological components: subjectivity, consciousness, and learning (Dilts, 1980). Subjectivity is the idea that all humans experience the world in unique and highly personal ways. No two people experience the same event in precisely the same way, and more importantly, those two people will assign very different emotional meaning to that experience. Subjective experiences are recalled or imagined using the five senses (Dilts, 1980). We rehearse speeches "in our heads" before going out on stage. When we remember crucial moments from the past, we 'see' and 'hear' the moment once more in our minds. When we're reading books or articles, we often create sensory images in our minds to correlate with the information we're taking in. According to NLP, each person's subjective representations of their own lives have a discernible structure or pattern. The images a person chooses when remembering or imagining aren't accidental, nor are they pure responses to external stimuli. Learning the patterns of an individual's subjective representations is called "the study of the structure of the subjective experience" (Dilts, 1980).

NLP maintains that a person's behaviour can be understood in terms of their subjective representational structures (Dilts, 1980). 'Behaviour' in this case, can mean both verbal and non-verbal communication, as well as encompasses behaviours that are both incompetent or maladaptive and effective or skilful. Manipulating or changing these sense-based representations, therefore, can cause a person to change their behaviour (Dilts, 1980).

Learning is a significant way that NLP practitioners successfully change their behaviour (Bandler & Grinder, 1979). NLP-style learning is based on an imitative process called 'modelling,' in which the practitioner methodically codifies and then reproduces an exemplar's movements or speech patterns. Doing this theoretically enables the practitioner to achieve expertise in any activity, even ones they have never tried before or in which they have no formal training (Bandler & Grinder, 1979).

NLP techniques are increasingly being applied in psychotherapy, persuasion, sales, negotiation, management training, sports, teaching, coaching, team building, and even public speaking (Johnson, 1990). Wherever it emerges, its purpose is to alter somehow the way the practitioner or an intended target thinks about a particular subject to influence their behaviour in a certain way.

Therapists, in particular, have found NLP techniques to be useful, especially as they seem to naturally complement other practices like solution-focused brief therapy. NLP encourages behaviour changes by using reframing techniques (Battino, 2006). Once the target's deep emotional associations with the behaviour change, the brain begins to process the behaviour differently physiologically, and thus changes the behaviour altogether (Battino, 2006). The shifting of emotional associations with certain behaviours is particularly beneficial for therapists, especially those working with people who struggle with severe mood and personality disorders (Battino, 2006).

Neuro-Linguistic Psychotherapy's popularity as a therapeutic and otherwise behaviour-influencing technique is growing in the western world (Experiential Constructivist Therapies Section, n.d.). In the United States, the method appears far more often in business settings, where several companies teach it as an advanced persuasion or negotiation tactic (Johnson, 1990).

The techniques and ideology behind NLP can be very quickly self-taught, and once mastered, there is no real need to pursue 'certification' to apply those techniques in your professional or personal life.

NLP AS AN ART

Perhaps it's more accurate to think of NLP as an art or a communicative skill. Though there are a variety of NLP techniques, all NLP interactions follow a basic pattern (Bandler & Grinder, 1979).

Establish Rapport (Bandler & Grinder, 1979)

The first stage in an NLP interaction is to establish rapport with the target. This is often achieved through pacing, or adjusting the speed at which the persuader speaks, and 'leading' or mimicking the target's verbal and non-verbal communications. Leading oral communications means identifying certain sensory predicates or keywords in the target's language. Which kinds of images do they tend to use when describing something? Is there a specific word or phrase that they use often? The persuader will adjust their speech patterns, using the same images and linguistic patterns that the client uses. Leading non-verbal communications involves mirroring the target's movements and responding to their eye movements. If the target crosses his legs, so will the persuader. If the target frequently runs a hand through her hair, then the persuader will start to do the same. If the target makes eye-contact, the persuader will meet it. If the target looks down at the floor when they talk, the persuader will start to do the same.

Mimic the target's language, and behaviour will make the target feel much more comfortable in the presence of the persuader. The familiarity of having their movements and language patterns repeated back to them will help them to relax and lull them into a sense of safety, security, and intimacy with the persuader.

Gather Information (Bandler & Grinder, 1979)

Once rapport has been established, the persuader can then start to collect information about the target's present problems and desired goals. Learning how the target perceives the current situation and understanding what the target wants the outcome of the situation to give the persuader the edge that they need to get what they want out of the conversation. However, an NLP practitioner isn't just seeking to determine what the target wants but is also listening for linguistic cues that tell the persuader what kinds of images the target associates with their desired outcome.

Make Interventions (Bandler & Grinder, 1979)

Once the persuader has learned the NLP's desired outcome and the current image-associates they have with that outcome, they can start to make small, linguistic interventions that shift the target's subjective image representations. In a negotiation or a manipulative situation, the influencer's task is to shift the target's image-associations from their own desired outcome to the desired outcome of the influencer. As the target's emotional responses to the desired outcome begin to shift, their behaviour and perspective on the situation will also start to change. Once their own emotional need for fulfilment and the image-structures that are connected with that need is fully transferred from their desired outcome to the influencer's desired result, then they will do what they can to achieve that outcome. In a therapeutic or personal situation, the influencer uses NLP techniques to shift the target's emotional responses to negative emotions like fear or insecurity as they are related to the desired goals.

Integrate Changes (Bandler & Grinder, 1979)

The final stage of an NLP interaction is for the influencer to prompt the target to visualise themselves, achieving their desired goals within the new framework of subjective image-associations that have been created for them by the influencer. In a persuasive or manipulative situation, this is the moment when the influencer can determine how successful they've been. Hearing the target verbalise their new intentions and goals confirms for the influencer how successful their programming has been. In a personal or therapeutic setting, the target is encouraged to return frequently to the new image-structures associated with the achievement of their goals until the desired objectives have been achieved in real life.

Not all NLP techniques follow these steps exactly. Adjustments are made depending on the situation, the influencer's intentions for using NLP on their target, and even for the nature of the target. Many organisations have developed their NLP techniques, and individual practitioners from around the world have used many different methods to implement NLP into their daily lives.

NLP is a flexible discipline, which makes it attractive to practitioners as it's a skill that you can continue to hone and develop throughout your lifetime. As you begin integrating NLP into your own life, you may choose to look for techniques that have been specifically designed for the types of situations you intend to use them in.

Remember also that NLP, like any art form, takes practice to perfect. Your first few attempts at NLP may be clumsy, but that's ok! The more you use it, the more you'll begin to develop your style, understanding which techniques work for you in which situations. You may even want to create a journal or other method for reflection. After each NLP interaction, record what worked and what didn't, perhaps making notes for how you can adjust your technique in the future.

There are many communities of practitioners who have found success using it in their personal and professional lives. If you wish to learn from other NLP practitioners or simply meet other like-minded people, these groups are often easy to find online. Many of them even conduct remote meetings or have chat functions on their websites, making it possible to connect with other practitioners from all over the world.

6

NLP – PRACTICAL APPLICATION AND

NLP FOR BEGINNERS

If you're new to NLP, there are a few simple techniques you can begin to employ in future conversations that may be difficult to navigate. You'll notice when they start to work, as you'll find people more and more willing to do what you ask without a struggle. NLP can also be used as a self-help tool, and so these techniques can be used to change your behaviour as well. As you become more confident, you can begin to add more and more advanced techniques to your repertoire.

Dissociation (Hurst, 2016)

NLP understands that emotions and behaviours are closely related to one another. For example, perhaps you have a negative encounter with an ex-girlfriend on your front porch. All of a sudden, you start coming in through the back door whenever you get home from work. Your negative emotional association with the front door has caused you to alter your behaviour subconsciously. Influencing another person's behaviour is often as simple as changing their psychological associations. To first change someone's emotional associations, you must first break the emotional relationships they already have.

Dissociation is a simple way to divorce someone from their emotions. If you want the other person to be happy, but notice that they've become nervous or anxious, you can employ a simple distraction to snap them out of their emotional state. Dropping a coin on the floor, for example, or setting the alarm to ring on your phone. Once the person's emotions have passed, you can resume the conversation from a neutral place.

Content Reframing (Hurst, 2016)

This technique is most helpful when you know what the other person wants from the conversation. For example, perhaps you're trying to convince your wife to quit smoking. But every time you bring it up, it turns into a fight. Content reframing simply means presenting an idea in a new or different light. If you always talk about smoking as bad for you, reframing the conversation would mean talking about smoking in a different context. This time, perhaps tell her about the friend of yours who was diagnosed with lung cancer and how they're stuck with the distressing choice of either not seeking treatment or leaving their family behind with massive medical debt. Now you're talking about the potential consequences of smoking as something that's affecting the decisions one faces and the lives of other loved ones around you that could be devastated. The context will lower your target's guard and open them up to suggestions that they were closed to before.

Anchoring (Hurst, 2016)

Anchoring involves using a simple physical stimulus to recreate a powerful emotional state. Physical touch is extremely effective as an anchor, but sounds can be useful as well. To anchor your target, wait for them to reach a heightened emotional state. Then, depending on your relationship with that person, you can either touch them with a simple gesture or make a particular sound. A hand on the shoulder is a very neutral way to touch someone, or maybe a pat on the back. Alternatively, you could tap your pen sharply on the table, or clear your throat loudly. For the rest of the conversation, if you want to bring your target back to that emotional state, simply repeat the anchor. This is a useful way to change the target's emotional associations with specific topics or ideas.

Building Rapport with Mirroring (Hurst, 2016)

This is the first stage in NLP, and for many practitioners, the only stage. Getting the target to feel relaxed and comfortable around you is often all you need to open them up to your suggestions. In addition to the usual ways, you would get someone to feel comfortable around you, try mirroring their movements. Sit or stand with the same posture. If they tilt their head, wait for a moment before tilting yours. If they smile, smile back. Mirroring helps people to feel comfortable around you because it makes you feel familiar. This technique is especially useful for strangers or people with whom you don't have a close relationship.

NLP Scripts (Hurst, 2016)

Many organisations and companies have written and published NLP 'scripts.' These are pre-planned words and phrases that you can use in specific conversations to help build rapport with the target and gain more information about their desired goals for the conversation. There are many NLP scripts available for free online for a variety of situations and industries, and there are thousands more that are available for purchase. These scripts are great for beginners because they can help you become more comfortable using NLP-style language. Rather than focusing on what to say, you can focus on how people respond to certain kinds of speech and phrasing. Before you know it, you'll be smoothly employing those phrases without the need to rely on a script.

Affirmations (Hurst, 2016)

Believe it or not, affirmations are also an NLP technique. When using them for self-transformation, an affirmation is a word, phrase, or even full statement that you repeat to yourself over and over until you believe them. An example of a personal affirmation might be something as long as "I am finally ready to make peace with my fears and move past them" or as simple as "I am a good person." If you repeat the phrase enough, you'll eventually believe it's true.

But you can use affirmations to influence others as well. It's the same concept, but instead of repeating the phrase over and over to yourself, you say it out loud to another person. If someone is saving up for something, you can remind them that "you're getting closer to your financial goal", or if you know that someone has been working out, you can tell them that they look healthier and fitter recently.

ADVANCED NLP

If you're already familiar with NLP, these techniques are a bit more advanced. They will require more practice to perfect, but they also tend to yield better results than the more straightforward methods. Most of these advanced practices have been developed for business and sales negotiations, but can be adapted to fit any conversation, both professional and personal.

Understand the Decision-Making Cycle (Beale, 2020)

When someone is making a decision, whether they're shopping online or sending out college applications, they typically go through a set of distinct cognitive phases. Understanding these phases can help you to apply your NLP strategies with more effectiveness and give you more control as you steer the other person toward making the decision that you want them to make.

The first step is **recognising a problem or opportunity**; it is at this moment when the person realises that they have a decision to make. In formal or professional conversations, this moment may have happened before the conversation ever started. If you're entering a pre-scheduled meeting or court case, for example, then the target has already recognised the problem or the opportunity at hand. However, in personal or sales contexts, this moment can be actively engineered using NLP. After you have engaged in rapport with the target, you can then present the situation to them. Rather than simply telling the other person what you want, giving it as a choice will be far more motivating for the target. For example, if you're a telemarketer and you'd like to organise a face-to-face meeting, instead of asking the target if he wants to meet in person, ask them if Monday or Tuesday works better for them.

The second step is **researching alternatives.** Anyone faced with a decision will want to consider all of the available options before making their final choice. NLP can be used at this stage to either recognise or create emotional associations with specific options. Of course, you want to build positive emotional associations with your desired outcome. You can use information that you've gained about your target's internal subjective experience structures to shift those structures onto your desired outcome, or positively anchor your target to a discussion of your desired outcome.

The third step is a **test** or trial run although this isn't an option for every decision, if it's possible to sample, preview, or test an opportunity before committing, most people will choose to do so. This is the ideal stage in which to create positive emotional and internal image associations with your desired outcome or even to develop negative emotional associations if your target chooses to preview an option that you don't want them to choose.

The fourth step is **making the decision.** At this point, you'll know how successful your programming techniques were throughout the conversation. If you have a long-standing relationship with this person, however, or if this decision is going to influence future decisions potentially, then you can still use this moment as an opportunity to influence your target. If the target made the choice you wanted them to make, you could reinforce their future compliance by creating positive emotional associations with the decision-making moment itself. If they ultimately did not make the choice you wanted them to make, then you can try to build negative emotional associations with the target's chosen outcome, perhaps even enough to influence them to change their mind at a later time.

Questions for Problem and Value Statements (Beale, 2020)

Before entering the conversation with your target, practice your answers to these questions. These will help you to prepare statements that will influence the target when addressing the problem and help you to assign value to specific options or outcomes that the target will then internalise.

- What do you have in common with the target? Establishing similarities furthers the physical mirroring you'll do in the room, making the target feel even more relaxed and connected to you. If you confirm that you are just like them, then they will be more likely to internalise your values and desired outcomes.

- What experiences, actions, or connections is the target likely to respect? If your target respects intelligence, then make sure you come off as intelligent. If the target appreciates physical attractiveness, spend some extra time in the mirror before your conversation. If the target values personal connections, make sure to name-drop when establishing rapport.

- What problems have you solved in the past that are relevant to the individual? These can be directly related to the conversation at hand, or they can be connected to other interests or areas of the target's life. Either way, indicating that you can solve problems they have will make them more eager to listen to and work with you.

- What solutions can you offer that are relevant to the target's problems? If you can reframe your desired outcome to appear as if it's the target's desired outcome, then they'll do whatever you wish. Alternatively, if you can frame your desired outcome as a clear solution to a problem that the target wishes to be solved, then they will also be far more likely to act as you want them to.

- What approaches or strategies can you offer? Indicating to the target that you can offer them some kind of exclusive help or support if they make a particular decision will make them far more likely to make that decision. Most people will act contrary to their desired outcome if it appears that achieving that outcome will be too difficult or that they will receive a lot more resources and support if they make a different decision.

NLP Script for Getting an Appointment, Meeting, or Audience (Beale, 2020)

Sometimes you have to use your influence simply to get someone to agree to meet with you in the first place! Scheduling appointments with demanding clients, meetings with elusive upper-level executives, or even cornering your husband who become mysteriously busy every time you try to talk to him about a sensitive subject can be difficult work for the average person. But there are specific NLP tactics you can use to convince the other person to agree to speak with you.

This script is designed for the appointment of arranging an appointment or business meeting, but with a slight adjustment, it can be used to set up more personal conversations as well:

Hello (their name), this is (your name) from (how do they know you?). Are you in a meeting or do you have 2 minutes right now?

It's essential to give the target options, rather than insisting that you schedule the appointment right now. Make them feel that they are choosing to listen to you and that if they didn't want to talk, they could simply say that they are busy. 2 minutes is also crucial. If you simply say "do you have time right now" the other person is likely to say no. But 2 minutes is nothing, right?

Thank you. I appreciate your time. Two minutes work well... *Only now tell your target why you want to arrange a time to speak with them.*

If you'd like to discuss this further, I'd be happy to arrange a 20-minute meeting to... *propose your desired outcome as if it's an option or opportunity worthy of the target's consideration.*

Will you be available to meet (suggest a time) or is there a time that works better for you?

Giving the target the option to set the meeting time themself will make them more likely to choose your time and will reinforce the idea that the client is a willing and active participant in arranging this meeting. Once the target agrees to the meeting time, thank them, confirm the details, and end the conversation as soon as is polite. The longer you talk, the more likely you are to lose your influence over the target.

DON'T BE A VICTIM OF NLP.

Even simple NLP tactics can give you a much-needed edge when negotiating with your boss for a higher salary or trying to convince your husband to take down that awful painting in the living room. But not all NLP practitioners have your best interests at heart. The technique is beloved by persuaders and negotiators, but it can also be put to devastating use by manipulators, dark personalities, and organisations. Whether you choose to learn its techniques or not, you should at least learn some basic ways to recognise when someone is using it on you so that you can defend yourself accordingly.

Be Wary of People Mimicking Your Body Language (Louv, n.d.)

You cross your arms, and just a few seconds later, they do too. You unconsciously adjust your glasses and then watch as they adjust theirs. One of the basics of NLP is mimicking the target's body movements to make them feel more relaxed and comfortable. If you suspect that someone is doing this to you, try making a few simple test gestures and see if the other person copies you. If they do, extricate yourself from the conversation as soon as possible.

Move Your Eyes in Unpredictable Patterns (Louv, n.d.)

To establish rapport, NLP practitioners will closely watch the way that their target's eyes move. They will do this for mimicry, but they are also learning how the target stores information. How do the target's eyes move when they're relaxed? Uncomfortable? Thinking hard? Lying? If you suspect that someone is watching your eyes to perform NLP, intentionally move your eyes in random or sporadic ways. This will be difficult for them to mimic, and it will be impossible for them to gather any more information on how your mind works.

Don't Let Strangers or Acquaintances Touch You (Louv, n.d.)

This is a good rule in general, but it's a fundamental way to protect yourself from NLP. A common NLP technique is to touch the target while they are in a heightened emotional state, perhaps putting a gentle hand on your shoulder if you're upset or 'accidentally' tapping your foot under the table when you burst out laughing at a joke they just told. This technique is called 'anchoring.' When you're in a highly emotional state, your body becomes much more sensitive to external stimuli. Touching you while you're in a highly emotional state is a way for the NLP influencer to create a subconscious association in your brain between that emotion and that specific way of being touched. For the rest of the conversation, if the influencer wants you to feel happy or sad, all they have to do is touch you the same way.

Notice Vague Language (Louv, n.d.)

NLP practitioners are mining your speech for specific words and symbols, which means that they're going to be very careful not to give you any of their own. If you feel that someone is intentionally using vague language to lull you into speaking more, try asking them questions. Be very wary of someone reluctant to provide you with specific details. Questions like "What colour was that car again?" or "God, I love the fall. What's your favourite part of fall?" are questions that require specific sensory words as answers. If the other person tries to wheedle their way without giving you any exact words, they are most likely trying to use NLP.

Notice Permissive Language (Louv, n.d.)

NLP is all about making the target feel relaxed and comfortable. It's about suggestion and subtle emotional associations. An NLP practitioner will never outright tell you to do something. Instead, they often use keywords or phrases that are designed to make you think that their suggestion was your idea. Phrases like "feel free to relax" or "you're welcome to try it out" should raise red flags. See what happens if you politely but firmly say no to these requests.

Insist on Full Participation (Louv, n.d.)

Similar to the use of vague language, NLP influencers will want to get your initial attention, and then slowly fade into the background as they gain more and more control over your thoughts and feelings. Don't let the other person get away with keeping things vague or constantly shifting the conversation back over to you. Questions like "Can you be more specific about that?" or "What exactly do you mean by that?" will force the influencer to reveal more of their intentions, and inhibit their ability to frame the conversation around you and your goals.

Listen Closely (Louv, n.d.)

NLP is based on language. When the influencer does speak, be very careful of odd turns of phrase. Skilled NLP practitioners choose every word with intention, and that intention is to influence your behaviour in some way. So, for example, if the influencer says "Diet and sleep with me are so critical to good health. Don't you agree?" that extra "with me" after sleep wasn't an accident, nor was it just a quirky way of phrasing the question. That's an image that's being intentionally planted in your mind as a future possibility.

Remain Fully Present (Louv, n.d.)

If you find yourself spacing or zoning out, terminate the conversation. NLP techniques are used to make you feel relaxed. A relaxed brain is much easier to influence, as you become more susceptible to suggestion, the more comfortable you are. If you're starting to space out during a conversation, that might mean that you're just a little tired this afternoon, but it can also indicate that your brain is falling prey to NLP relaxation techniques. If you've gotten to this point, do everything you can to wake yourself up. Ask your conversation partner if they'd be interested in a cup of coffee. Excuse yourself to go to the bathroom and take a quick walk to get your blood flowing. While you're spaced out, your influencer will make suggestions that will influence your behaviours and beliefs in the future–ideas that you might be too out of it even to remember.

7

BODY LANGUAGE

People are always talking, even when they're silent. As much as 60% of human communication is non-verbal (Fremont College, 2018). We are continually sending other people subliminal messages with our facial expressions, posture, arms, and even eye movements. Much of this communication happens subconsciously (Fremont College, 2018). We may not be aware of the signals that other people are sending us, but our brains are wired to pick them up and respond in kind. Subtle cues in body language are often responsible for the problematic 'feelings' we get about people. Someone might just give you a creepy feeling or seem inherently trustworthy, but you can't quite explain what is making you feel this way.

Body language encompasses all parts of the body, including facial expressions, posture, gestures, eye movement, touch, and even the use of space (Fremont College, 2018). There is much debate about whether or not body language is universal, as certain gestures and movements can vary in meaning from culture to culture. However, there are many gestures and actions that seem to be familiar with almost every human society. Those who study body language typically (and understandably) focus on the norms within their own culture, but learning the subtle differences among cultures can significantly enhance your ability to communicate with people across ethnic and national lines (Fremont College, 2018).

The formal study of body language is called kinesics, and it is such an intricate field that there are several subcategories (Brown, 2005). Oculesics is the study of eye movement, and specifically how eye movement is used to communicate and express emotions (Sullivan, 2009). Haptics is the study of touch and how it's used as an interpersonal and communicative tool (Author, 2013). Oculesics and haptics tend to see a great deal of variety across ethnic lines, but they can also present with variation across lines of gender, age, and even socioeconomic class (Author, 2013).

Haptics itself is further divided into situational categories, as the way we use touch to communicate changes dramatically depending on the nature of the conversation we are having. The five haptic types are functional/professional, social/polite, friendship/warmth, love/intimacy, and sexual/arousal (Author, 2013). Using touch signals from an intimacy category that doesn't match the current situation can potentially come across to the other person as threatening or cold. For example, touching a co-worker the way you would touch a friend might make your co-worker feel extremely uncomfortable while using the appropriate touch signals for social/polite situations with a romantic partner might make you seem distant or socially unavailable (Author, 2013).

Proxemics, another subcategory of body language study, deals with the way that people use space (Hall, 1990). Proxemics, like haptics, is also divided into four intimacy categories: intimate, personal, social, and public (Hall, 199). These categories are used to describe the distance at which people stand from each other while communicating in certain situations. Changing the distance between you and your conversation partner can convey several things, including the desire for intimacy, the desire for conflict, rejection, or fear (Hall, 1990).

Though it's not often categorised with "body language," tone of voice is another form of non-linguistic communication (Bodylanguageuniversity.com, 2019). Typically, the tone of voice matches body language, not necessarily the words that are being used. For example, if you are angry, but tell your conversation partner that you are fine, your body language and tone will both follow patterns that convey anger, even though the words you're speaking say that you're feeling fine. Specific postures can change a person's tone of voice, as they can restrict or open the airways. Generally speaking, sitting or standing with a hunched posture restricts the airways, and can make your vocal tone sound muffled or muted. In turn, this can sometimes indicate to another person that you are tired or unhappy, even if that's not necessarily the truth. On the flip side, speaking with a straight back opens the airways and gives your vocal tone more colour and expression (Bodylanguageuniversity.com, 2019).

Learning to read body language can reveal a great deal about the people around us. Body language is our primary indicator of attitude. It's estimated that in a conversation dealing with feelings or beliefs, only 7% of communication is conveyed through language, 38% is the tone of voice, and 55% is done through body language (Mehrabian, 2009). Though these numbers vary slightly from study to study, it's commonly accepted by most cognitive scientists and psychologists that more than half of human communication is done through body language (Mehrabian, 2009).

Learning to read body language reveals the actual attitudes and feelings of the people around us. But learning to alter our body language is a powerful tool for social influence, perhaps even the most powerful tool we have. Master manipulators and persuaders alike intentionally change their body language to make the other person believe certain things about them. Even the most vicious abusers can appear friendly and charming and put the people around them entirely at ease. While some of their tricks are based on words, most of the manipulative work is being done through body language. Good manipulators and persuaders also know how to read the body language of their target, so that they can respond to the target's true inner feelings without giving away anything that they are thinking. Body language can help to give you an edge in business dealings, conversations with volatile or ambiguous people. It can even help to make you more sexually appealing to potential partners.

BECOMING FLUENT – HOW TO READ BODY LANGUAGE OF PERSUASION

While certain parts of the body are difficult to control, certain gestures are natural to fake or mimic. Mastering these gestures can give you an edge in a variety of social settings, conveying what you want to say and masking your true feelings or attitudes.

Facial Expressions (Kurien, 2010)

Facial expressions do quite a lot of communicative work, arguably as much as the rest of the body combined. Movements of the eyes, eyebrows, lips, nose, and cheeks can all connect in different ways to convey different mood states and emotions.

A facial expression that's nearly impossible to fake is a genuine smile. When people smile with joy, small crinkles from around their eyes, if someone is faking their smile, the skin around their eyes will be smooth and wrinkle-free. Before engaging in a fake smile, many people grimace slightly before putting on the fake smile. A half-smile only engages one corner of the mouth, and typically indicates sarcasm or uncertainty. Tight or pursed lips show displeasure. The more relaxed someone's mouth is, the more relaxed and positive their attitude is. Covering the mouth or touching the lips while speaking is an indicator that the other person is lying.

The eyes alone do a great deal of communicative work and are especially good indicators of true feelings because we have very little control over them. The pupils of the eye will expand or retract, depending on how interested someone is in a particular topic. If the person you're speaking with is interested and engaged, their pupils will dilate slightly. If they are bored or disinterested, then their pupils will contract.

Humans blink around 6-10 times per minute. However, the urge to blink is slowed when we encounter someone that we find physically or sexually attractive. Though old movies show Hollywood starlets batting their eyelashes at their love interests, the reality is that the more attracted you are to someone, the less you blink when talking to them. On the other hand, blinking rate increases when someone is stressed or thinking rapidly. Because racing thoughts increase blinking rate, an increased blink rate is a significant indicator that someone is lying, especially when it's accompanied by touching the face.

Eye contact is also a significant communicative indicator. Refusal to make eye contact can indicate several things, but it depends on what direction the eyes move in. If someone refuses to meet your eyes but looks somewhere else, this can indicate boredom or disinterest. It can also suggest that the other person is lying to you. Typically, people tend to look off to the right if they're lying, and off to the left if they recall an actual memory. If a person looks down, however, this indicates feelings of nervousness or submissiveness.

Glancing at something and then looking away very quickly indicates a desire for that person or thing. Glancing at the door, for example, can indicate a desire to leave the room or escape the conversation, while glancing at a person can indicate a willingness to talk with that person.

Head and Neck Gestures (Fremont College, 2018)

Nodding the head is generally an indicator of consent, agreement, or approval. A single nod of the head can be used to acknowledge another person's presence when they enter a room. Some studies believe that this is a muted, Western variant of the full-body bow practised in many Asian cultures as a formal greeting. Shaking the head, on the other hand, typically indicates refusal, disapproval, or disagreement. In India and other southern Asian cultures, tilting the head slightly from side to side is an indicator of understanding or approval.

Lowering both the head and the eyes is an indicator of submission while raising the head from a lowered posture can indicate a renewed interest in the conversation. Tilting the head to one side is also an expression of interest. It can also show curiosity, uncertainty, or even confusion. If the head is propped up by the hand while it's tilted, this can be an indicator that the other person is in deep thought, but it can also be a sign of disinterest. If the head is tilted forward slightly, this is an indicator that the other person is feeling suspicious or sceptical.

General Body Postures (Mondloch, Nelson, & Horner, 2013)

When someone is sitting with their back straight or leaning forward slightly, this is an indicator that they are feeling both relaxed and interested in the conversation. Crossing the legs or the arms, on the other hand, indicates impatience or disinterest in the conversation.

If the feet are both pointed toward the speaker, this is typically an indicator that the other person is feeling relaxed, open, and engaged. Putting the hands on the hips, especially in men, can indicate a sexual attraction to the person with whom they are speaking.

. When someone's chest is pointed toward the speaker, it indicates feelings of confidence. When a straight back accompanies this, this shows extreme feelings of confidence and social prominence. A hunched back and shoulders, on the other hand, indicates a lack of confidence.

Positioning the chest close to another person, so that you are standing face-to-face close to each other, can either be a sign of deep engagement in the conversation or a sign of assertiveness and aggression.

Placing a hand over the heart indicates sincerity or great depth of feeling. Rubbing the chest, on the other hand, is a sign of tension, stress, or discomfort.

Shoulders (Fremont College, 2018)

Shoulders are a highly expressive part of the body and one that we have a lot of control over. Shoulder movements are often involuntary, but if you can become aware of how your shoulders are moving in social situations, you can make adjustments to convey or hide certain emotions.

Rolling the shoulders back is a sign of confidence, especially with a straight back. If you want other people to see you as confident, keep your shoulders back and your back straight. Even if you feel nervous or insecure, this simple posture will change the way people perceive and interact with you. Rolling the shoulders forward is a sign of low confidence and self-esteem. If you're trying to hide your confidence or come across as meeker than you are, try slouching or hunching your shoulders.

The more relaxed someone is, the lower their shoulders sit. Tension and anxiety cause the shoulders to rise toward the ears. If you want to appear comfortable, keep your shoulders sitting as low as possible. Check your shoulders if you feel yourself becoming tense or anxious.

Shoulders often contribute to first impressions. Strong and flexible shoulders indicate strength and vitality, while small, stiff shoulders can sometimes indicate depression. These impressions are quick and unconscious and may have nothing at all to do with the person's other mannerisms. If you want to give the impression of strength and vitality, exercises that open and strengthen the shoulders can dramatically change the way people perceive you, even if there's no discernible difference in your size or body shape.

Gestures (Kurien, 2010)

Gestures made with the hands, arms, fingers, head, and legs are all movements that, when we become aware of them, we can adjust to gain more control over the way we present ourselves in conversation. Folded or crossed arms are rarely seen as a welcoming gesture and often indicates to the other person that you aren't listening to what they have to say. If you want to seem open, friendly, and interested, make sure that your arms stay by your sides or even in your pockets. If you're going to end a conversation early, on the other hand, crossed arms may give the other person a hint that you're not interested.

Tension is also stored in the hand. Relaxed hands indicate confidence or self-assurance, while clenched fists signify stress or anger. If you want others to see you as cool and calm, try to keep your hands open and relaxed, even if you're secretly fuming. If you do want the other person to see that you're angry, however, a clenched fist is a much better signal than shouting. Wringing the hands indicates nervousness and anxiety. If you're feeling nervous, do your best to keep your hands still, and others won't realise just how anxious you are.

Handshakes (Fremont College, 2018)

A handshake might seem like a simple, innocent greeting, but it's a crucial moment of communication. Grabbing the person's fingers rather than their palm can indicate nervousness while squeezing the other person's hand too firmly can either show insecurity or aggression. Shaking hands too weakly can suggest to the other person that you're not interested in them or emotionally invested in the conversation. Refusing to make eye contact while shaking hands can be a sign of nervousness or submission. When you move in to shake hands, a firm, friendly handshake with eye contact is the best way to signal to the other person that you are confident, but not aggressive. A good handshake can do a lot of psychological work to make the other people feel more relaxed around you, while a lousy handshake can do a lot to start a meeting off on the wrong foot.

Breathing (Covey, Tracy, & Hamilton, 2009)

Rhythms of breath have a direct relationship to our stress levels. But in addition to calming you down, deep, even breathing conveys the impression of relaxation and confidence to other people. Before you start to feel the effects of deep breathing, the people around you will respond to the social cues it sends. If you start to feel nervous or anxious, make an effort to regulate your breathing. This will help you to keep calm, but it will also ensure that no one around you sees the actual level of your anxiety.

Mirroring another person's breathing pattern is a way to establish intimacy and familiarity with another person. Breathing in sync with another person will make them feel relaxed and emotionally connected with you, and that, in turn, will make them feel much more comfortable around you.

Physical Movements (Fremont College, 2018)

Not fully formed gestures, small physical movements can still do a lot of communicative work in social situations. Avoid touching your mouth as it can indicate that you're hiding or lying about something.

8

PERSUASION – PROFESSIONAL VS. PERSONAL

Persuasion and manipulation can look slightly different depending on whether the setting is personal or professional. Tactics that are effective or even ethical in a business meeting may not work as well in a conversation between married partners. The methods that a salesperson uses when persuading a client to close a deal may be entirely ethical at work, but aggressive enough to be considered manipulative if used to influence a romantic partner to move in with them. The social rules change in professional and personal situations. Intentions change, as does the delicate balance between personal gain and harming another. It's far more common to use persuasion tactics for the benefit of another in personal settings. At the same time, this kind of altruism is rare in a professional environment and may even be considered a betrayal of the organisation for whom you work.

Many of the tactics spoken about in this book so far have equal application in both professional and personal settings. Brainwashing almost always happens on a 'professional' or organisational level, while mind control is far more common in interpersonal relationships. Both are examples of manipulative conformity at its worst.

But the rules of conformity also change depending on whether the setting is professional or personal. Most of us don't question that a company has the right to determine what we can wear and how we behave. If a company tells us to remove your facial piercings, we rarely feel that we've been manipulated or that our autonomy has been violated. But when your parents tell you that you can't wear facial piercings in their house, this can feel like an attack. And it becomes an outright psychological attack if your parents stop speaking to you after you show up with a facial piercing or make comments in your presence about how facial piercings look tacky without implicating you directly.

The lines between professional and personal can also become blurred in the workplace. If you consider your co-workers your friends, then is your relationship with them, personal or professional? Persuasion is an integral part of management training, as it is one of the primary responsibilities of leaders and supervisors to motivate employees, give directions, and facilitate operations in the workplace. It's far healthier to persuade your employees to make changes or take on new responsibilities than it is to force them. However, leaders and supervisors can very easily cross the line from persuasion to manipulation. Due to workplace hierarchies and the social expectations of an employer/employee relationship, however, this manipulation can be challenging to spot from the outside. Were the employee and the employer equals within the company, or if they had a personal relationship outside of the workplace, then it would be much more evident that the employer's behaviour is indeed manipulative. But the social structures that support authority and workplace obedience, unfortunately, make it very easy for manipulators to thrive in professional settings. This is why dark triad personality traits make it more likely that someone will receive a promotion, and why these personality types are disturbingly over-represented in the upper-management and CEO levels of business.

Understanding how social influence works and changes in professional and personal settings can help you to both succeed in your relationships and recognise when someone around you is manipulative. Understanding the psychology of business negotiations can make you better at your job. It can help you to know when the person across the table from you stops persuading and starts manipulating. Understanding the psychology of workplace hierarchies can help you identify when a co-worker or supervisor is manipulating you and can help you to defend yourself against their attacks. Learning the difference between professional and personal negotiations can also make you a much better conversationalist outside of work. Learning which tactics are appropriate for interpersonal conversations will make you much more persuasive and improve your communications with strangers and loved ones alike.

Human beings are inherently social creatures. There are 'rules" to all social situations, professional and personal alike. In professional settings, the rules are typically articulated more clearly, while they can sometimes be murkier in personal settings. For example, a brilliant lawyer can find it very difficult to have even the most candid discussion with their partner. Or a college student can effortlessly charm every person they date but find themselves stuttering and stammering their way through a job interview. Some persuasion tactics are universal. Body language, in particular, changes very little between social settings. But social situations, levels of intimacy, and even personality types all combine to determine the 'rules' of every conversation. Social influence is inherently social, and therefore, if the social rules and expectations change, then so make the rules of social influence.

The essential step in becoming influential is learning that there is no universal way to be persuasive (Cialdini, 1984). The best persuaders and manipulators learn how to read social situations and adjust their behaviours accordingly. Unfortunately, this quality comes much more naturally to manipulators than it does to persuaders. Manipulative people are seeking to gain something from every social interaction, and so are more naturally attuned to the social cues they receive from the people around them. They feel no need to represent themselves honestly, and so don't hesitate to mould themselves to fit in whatever social situation they happen to be. Persuaders, however, can learn to do this effectively as well. A good persuader will learn how to adjust their behaviour to fit the social situation without compromising their personality or feeling the need to present themselves dishonestly (Cialdini, 1984).

PROFESSIONAL MANIPULATION

In general, aggressive persuasion tactics are far more socially acceptable in professional settings than they are in personal ones. The reason for this is transparency. When walking into a negotiation, both parties understand that persuasion tactics are going to be used.

When listening to a sales pitch or sitting in court, you are essentially consenting to be persuaded. The mutual understanding and expectation that persuasion is going to be used to allow for more sophisticated methods to be used without crossing the line into manipulation. The social rules of a negotiation necessitate persuasion and therefore permit more advanced forms of it (Cialdini, 1984).

In 1984, Dr Robert Cialdini completely changed the culture of business negotiation when he published his book *Influence: The Psychology of Persuasion*. In this book, he outlined six "weapons of persuasion" that can be used to close almost any business deal successfully. Though he refers to them as 'weapons,' application of these tactics is rarely considered manipulation, primarily because they all use natural, psychological responses to convince the other party to listen to the influencer. They don't, on the other hand, trick or force the target into making a particular decision.

1. Reciprocity

When someone gives something to us, we feel naturally inclined to return the favour. Some personality types wish to repay a perceived act of kindness, while others simply dislike feeling indebted to someone else. Websites and businesses use this tactic all the time to stunning effect. How much more likely are you to sign up for a newsletter or mailing list if, in return, you've been offered something like a discount or free merchandise? This is a marketing tactic, intended to inspire purchases and customer loyalty, but it's considered persuasion because it hides nothing from the customer. You know what the company wants from you. The offer of reciprocity simply makes you more likely to say 'yes.'

In a negotiation, this principle is applied in the form of making a concession. When first called upon to make an offer or request, the influencer makes a substantial request, asking for much more than they need or want. When the target refuses, the persuader then makes a smaller request as a counteroffer, which the target is far more likely to accept because it appears that you're making some kind of compromise. This tactic is persuasion in negotiations because the target always has the power to refuse. It's manipulation, however, if there is any implication that refusal will bring negative consequences to the target.

2. Social Proof

Essentially, this is an ethical application of conformity. If you can demonstrate that your product or service is accessible and helpful, then other people will be more willing to take part. People are far more likely to walk into a coffee shop or restaurant that's crowded with happy customers than they are to walk into a coffee shop that seems empty.

Soliciting and displaying customer reviews is the primary way in which businesses make use of this principle, and it's incredibly useful. Studies have demonstrated that nearly 70% of people read customer reviews before making a purchase online. 'Likes' and 'reposts' on social media serve a similar purpose. The more likes you have, the more influence you have.

Social proof speaks to our innate human need to belong to a group or community. Doing something that's against the grain is contrary to our nature, even if it's necessary or right. Convincing a customer, client, or fellow executive that making a particular decision has little social risk for them will make them far more likely to do as you ask. And if you believe that what you have to give is valuable, then it's not manipulation, it's persuasion.

3. Commitment and Consistency

No one wants to appear flaky and unreliable. Persuading someone to make some kind of public commitment will make them far more likely to follow through on their promises. This is why bringing up previous engagements is such an effective negotiation tactic. Reminding the person across the table of a time in the past when they invested in your company or expressed interest in buying makes them far more likely to repeat that action now. By invoking previous commitment, you're asking the other person to remain consistent. If they refuse, they're now going to be in the position of explaining why they've decided to change their behaviour.

This is also the primary component behind branding and selling 'merch.' Wearing a band t-shirt is a public statement of support for that band and makes you far more likely to listen to their music and attend their concerts in the future. Buying a travel mug from Starbucks is a public admission that you buy your coffee from Starbucks, and so makes you more likely to go back when you're craving your morning caffeine instead of choosing another coffee shop. This might seem insidious, but it's not manipulation, it's persuasion because the customer's right to choose is never in question. If you buy a travel mug at Starbucks and get your morning coffee from Dunkin' Donuts, Starbucks isn't going to punish or ostracise you. You're motivated to return to Starbucks from a need to remain reliable and consistent, not from a need to avoid punishment.

4. Liking

We're far more likely to listen to people that we like. This is why establishing rapport is such an essential part of professional dealings. From life in the office to rules of respect in a courtroom, many professional regulations and policies concerning behaviour are about easing and facilitating communications between many different kinds of people. When your supervisor greets you with a smile in the morning and asks you how your weekend was, he's trying to make you feel comfortable and relaxed around him. The more comfortable you are, the more likely you are to follow his directions.

This is why tactics like mirroring and finding commonalities are so important. Meeting strangers puts us on our guard. But when we realise that the other person has something in common with us, it makes us feel less nervous. Commonalities make the other person feel familiar and therefore make you feel more comfortable. Getting someone to feel comfortable and relaxed around you is considered persuasion if you don't intend to do the other person harm. If you want to take advantage, on the other hand, then this is manipulation. Making someone feel safe around you when they shouldn't be is representing yourself and your intentions dishonestly.

5. Scarcity

Something that is about to vanish or disappear is far more attractive to us than things that are in plentiful supply. This is why we value antiques or uniqueness. We like the idea of things that are rare and difficult to find. This trait is a survival tactic, hardwired into us from our days of hunting and gathering. We've evolved to notice and appreciate things that are in short supply so that we can take advantage of the opportunity.

Most humans are no longer hunter-gatherers, but good persuaders know that our brains still work this way. How many times have you stopped for a sales sign that said: "Limited Time Only"? It's not manipulation—there may very well be a limited supply, or the particular sale may indeed have a time limit. But it's persuasion to advertise it because it's scarcity alone will make the offer more attractive to another person.

What scientists call "loss aversion" is the underlying human belief that it's safer to avoid risk than it is to make gains. Reminding someone of what they stand to lose if they don't do as you ask is far more powerful than showing them what they promise to gain. While this might feel like making threats, if the decision-making power of the target is respected, then it's firmly persuasion. But if the things the target stands to lose are things like their personal safety, dignity, or autonomy, then this is not persuasion, but manipulation.

6. Authority

Last, but certainly not least, is the principle of authority. Humans have an ingrained respect for social hierarchies. This is a cooperative survival strategy, enabling us to work together within specific social systems. Using your authority to persuade others to do as you ask is not inherently unethical. If you are a leader or a supervisor, then others can and should do as you request, provided that what you're asking doesn't compromise their safety or dignity. And while it can be galling, it's not unethical or abusive for an authority figure to invoke their authority to demand compliance from you. Reminding people of your authority can be a powerful, persuasive tactic in any professional setting. Even if you aren't a boss or a CEO, reminding others of your associations with an expert, a celebrity, or another respected figure in the field can be a powerful way to influence their decisions and lend you credibility.

If, on the other hand, someone uses their authority as justification for making you do something that may harm you or make you uncomfortable, then this is no longer persuasion–it's manipulation. This is why it's never appropriate for supervisors to have sexual relationships with their subordinates, or for doctors to have intimate personal relationships with their patients. Authority gives you a great deal of power and a great deal of influence. Using that influence to get people to do things that they wouldn't normally do is absolutely manipulation, and it's not to be tolerated. If an authority figure uses their authority to make you do something you simply don't like doing, then that's, unfortunately, their right. But if they use their authority to make you do something that compromises your safety, dignity, or autonomy in any way, then they are manipulating you, and what they have done is unethical, regardless of the company's official policies or position.

PERSONAL MANIPULATION

In interpersonal relationships, the 'rules' change slightly. We have very different social expectations from our friends and families than we do from our bosses and co-workers. The way we behave at a party is very different from the way that we act at a board meeting. As such, the kinds of persuasion tactics that are acceptable also changes. Aggressive persuasion tactics like invoking authority or implying scarcity are far less acceptable in interpersonal relationships than they are in business negotiations. Even persuading someone to do something by suggesting that you'll like or even love them more if they do as you ask is not only considered manipulative, it can be regarded as emotional abuse (Simon, 2010).

But that being said, persuasion still exists on an inter-personal level (Cialdini, 1984). We persuade people to enter into more intimate relationships with us. We persuade people to like and love others. We persuade people into behaving specific ways, saying certain things, and believing in specific ideas. It's not a bad thing. At least, not if it's done with respect for the other person's safety, dignity, and right to choose. We always try to make positive decisions for those we love and care about, but sometimes, those decisions come into conflict with our ability to make positive decisions for ourselves. It's at this crossroads that we often find ourselves using persuasion. Picking fights and denying yourself the things you need in the name of being 'honest' or 'forthright' is hardly a healthy approach to your relationships. In many ways, using persuasion to get what you want is more honest than keeping your needs to yourself (Cialdini, 1984).

Non-verbal forms of communication are essential in all persuasive settings, but they're particularly crucial in interpersonal interactions (Cialdini, 1984). You may have no choice but to speak freely and honestly about a topic that you know is volatile. But your body language, appearance, and tone of voice when you enter that conversation can drastically change the way that the other person responds. The other person can receive the same words with different body language in very different ways. If you want to avoid a fight, study and practice postures, gestures, and eye movements that will make the other person feel calm and relaxed. If you need to go on the defence to make someone leave you alone, a simple change in posture or proximity can also save you from an altercation while accomplishing your goal of telling the other person that you no longer want them in your space (Cialdini, 1984).

Persuasion tactics save jobs, marriages, friendships, and family relationships all the time (Cialdini, 1984). Persuasion makes compromises easier and can strengthen communications and trust between people. Persuasion is often necessary for cooperation, as long as the tactics used are appropriate and respectful. It's when persuasion tactics are used to harm or control another person that they become harmful and manipulative (Cialdini, 1984).

It's relatively clear why influencing someone to do something that may put them in harm's way is unethical. Where interpersonal persuaders often accidentally cross the line into manipulation is when they try to control other people. Imagine that your daughter is trying to make it in a career that she's passionate about, but she's not making very much money. You think that she's wasting her time. You can see that she has so many other talents, and you know that she could be successful in so many different fields. But rather than have an honest conversation with her, you decide to use persuasion tactics to get her to quit her job and look for something else. You might mean well, but this would be considered a manipulative act. You may think you're doing something good for her daughter, and that by influencing her, you're helping to guide her toward the 'right' decision. But the problem with this is that you're assuming that you know what the 'right' decision is. Rather than telling your daughter honestly how you feel and trying your best to support her or find ways to help her succeed at what she loves, you've simply decided to take control of her behaviour. The reason that influencing your daughter to abandon her passion is manipulation is because doing so would violate her right to make her own choices. The moment that you lose respect for the other person's right to choose, you've tipped over from persuasion to manipulation (Simon, 2010).

Remember, in a professional setting; everyone is on the same page. If you go into a sales pitch or are attending a staff meeting, you understand that persuasion tactics are going to be used. Furthermore, everyone else expects that you will be using persuasion tactics yourself. But in an intimate conversation with a romantic partner, that's not necessarily an expectation. Partners, friends, and even strangers you meet at parties have invested a certain level of trust in you. If you use aggressive, persuasive tactics to control their attitudes or behaviours, then you have violated that trust because you've decided that your needs are more important than theirs (Simon, 2010).

Though the word 'manipulative' has become a bit of a buzzword in recent years, the term is often used to refer to people who are pushy or selfish (Simon, 2010). The real test of a manipulative person, however, is to see how they react when you say 'no.' A pushy person may push, but they will back off once they see that 'no' really does mean 'no.' Your relationship with this person may continue to be difficult, but you know that they still respect your right to make your own decisions. A manipulative person doesn't accept 'no.' Their way around your 'no' may be obvious, or it may be subtle. Still, if you find yourself continually being guilted, cajoled, bribed, or otherwise convinced to do something that you explicitly said you did not want to do, then you have a manipulative person on your hands. That person doesn't respect your right to make your own decisions. When you say 'no,' they simply change their tactics until that 'no' turns into a 'yes' (Simon, 2010).

9

HOW TO RECOGNISE AND DEFEND AGAINST CONTROLLING AND HIGHLY MANIPULATIVE PEOPLE

When you describe what manipulation is, it sounds obvious. Simple, even. But manipulation is very subtle. The better the manipulator, the harder they are to catch. Those who have been manipulated often don't realise what's happening to them, because manipulators are very good at making the other person feel responsible for their feelings. Dark triad personalities are especially good at making their targets feel responsible for things that are out of their control or guilty for things that aren't crimes or even flaws (Simon, 2010).

Manipulation is a form of deception (Simon, 2010). Manipulators are very good at sounding like they care for you, but the reality is that they only care for themselves. Dark personalities will manipulate simply for the fun of it. Other kinds of people will manipulate for personal power and gain. A widespread reason people employ manipulative tactics is to stop the people around them from behaving in a way that they disapprove of (Simon, 2010).

Almost all manipulation, especially interpersonal manipulation, is guilt-based (Simon, 2010). Making the other person feel like they have done something wrong or have something to make up for is a powerful psychological weapon. Humans are inherently cooperative creatures. If we feel that we've somehow wronged someone else, our instinct is to feel bad and to feel like we need to make up for what we've done. This is Dr Cialdini's 1st principle of persuasion, reciprocity, but twisted in a very malicious way.

The forms that manipulation takes will vary depending on the motive and personality of the manipulator, the personality of the target, and the social situation (Simon, 2010). However, there are specific common tactics that many manipulative people employ at one point or another. Learning to recognise these tactics can help you to spot manipulative people before they get too much out of you and can help you to confirm whether or not someone in your life is manipulative.

The most potent weapon that you have against manipulative and controlling people is one of the smallest words in our language – 'no.' Manipulators will do everything they can to get around that word. They might try to make you feel guilty or unreasonable for putting your foot down. But the reality is that making decisions that are good for you is never unreasonable or selfish. Those who love you will understand and respect when you have to put your foot down and set firm boundaries. Manipulative people, on the other hand, don't respect your autonomy, and so won't listen when you try to set boundaries with them (Simon, 2010).

Outside of setting firm boundaries, however, there are other ways that you can combat manipulative tactics when they're used against you. Saying 'no' can be difficult even with people that we love and respect, never mind to someone who is going to do whatever they can to make you say 'yes.' And if you're dealing with a dark personality, it might even be dangerous to refuse them too firmly (Simon, 2010).

Not everyone who is manipulative has a dark personality type (Simon, 2010). And not everyone who is manipulative is necessarily toxic. At one point or another, most of us will slip from persuasion into outright manipulation. Young children are perhaps the best manipulators of all because they haven't yet learned how to evaluate the consequences of their actions. But if someone persistently defies your boundaries or convinces you to do things that ultimately weren't good for you, then that person does need to be kept at a safe emotional distance. Even people with dark triad personality traits manage to have successful relationships with other people. But anyone that puts you in danger should be eliminated from your life as soon as it is safe to do so. If you want to let that person back into your life at a later date, that's up to you. But someone who doesn't respect your safety will eventually put you in harm's way. And if that person is manipulative, they will most likely convince you that it was your fault should any harm befall you (Simon, 2010).

Depending on how manipulative someone is, you may not have to cut them out of your life altogether (Simon, 2010). But recognising when and how they are manipulative will protect you from their influence and stop you from being taken advantage. If the manipulative person in your life is a family member, you may want to enlist the help of other members of the family. The same is true if this person is a co-worker or part of a friend group. Manipulators are very sensitive to social dynamics, often more so than other kinds of people. If they can sense that their tactics aren't working, they will change their course. The more people in your social group that are aware of their manipulative behaviour, the less they will be able to get away with (Simon, 2010).

Perhaps the most toxic situation with a manipulator is a romantic relationship (Simon, 2010). If your romantic partner is consistently manipulative or controlling, you may need to break off ties with them until they can learn to manage their manipulative behaviour better. If you are married to this person, however, you should enlist help from your family, close friends, or even members of your partner's family. The more witnesses you have to this person's behaviour, the safer you will be. This is especially important if you have children with this person, as manipulative people don't necessarily change their behaviour when dealing with young children. Dark triad personalities can be especially dangerous around children since their lack of empathy prevents them from taking the same kind of care with young children than other kinds of people (Simon, 2010).

RECOGNISING PSYCHOLOGICAL ATTACKS

Manipulation is an attack. In one way or another, it violates your safety, your dignity, and your autonomy. While there are as many manipulative strategies as there are manipulators, there are a few standard tactics to keep an eye out. If you recognise these behaviour patterns in someone around you, then you almost certainly are dealing with a manipulative person.

The Scared Routine (Sommer, n.d.)

Manipulative people don't always come across as sophisticated, charming, or powerful. A classic manipulative move is making you feel like *you're* the one overpowering *them*. When you call people out on their manipulative behaviour, one of the first things they will do is apologise. Profusely. They're sorry for whatever they did or said that made you upset. They're often sorry *because* they had some kind of bad experience in the past, and they reacted badly. They're sorry because they're scared that you're going to leave them.

The trouble with this kind of behaviour is that it absolves them of any responsibility for their actions. 'Triggers' are certain situations that make someone feel uncomfortable or distressed because they force the person to relive a previously traumatic experience. When triggered, people can behave strangely and even terribly. However, it's still not an excuse for someone to make you feel unsafe. When listening to an apology, listen very carefully. Is the other person sorry for hurting you or scaring you? Or are they sorry because you're calling them out on their unacceptable behaviour?

This tactic is particularly common in abusive romantic relationships. One partner will become extremely jealous, punishing, or hurtful when the other partner spends meaningful time with friends or family. Never allow anyone to separate you from your loved ones, as isolation is a classic manipulation strategy. Remember, manipulators are very sensitive to social pressure. The more witnesses they have, the less likely they are to manipulate.

Instilling Self-Doubt (Sommer, n.d.)

Manipulators make you feel like you're crazy or unreasonable. They make you feel like they have your best interests at heart. They make you feel like your feelings are unjustified or that your instincts are invalid. The moment you stop trusting yourself, that's when you become most vulnerable to their influence.

Resist this. If you feel like something is wrong, then something is wrong. It may not be what you think it is. But our instincts are good. Human brains are incredibly sophisticated at sensing danger. Now it's just your job to figure out what that 'something' really is.

The more manipulative the other person is, the better they are at making you doubt yourself. They might say something, and then later deny having said it. They will explain away behaviours that you would typically find unacceptable and justify things that don't sit right with you. Be very careful around anyone who makes you feel 'crazy.' You're not. If you feel that something is wrong, then something is wrong.

Avoiding Responsibility (Sommer, n.d.)

Manipulators make you feel like their feelings are your responsibility. We all have moments when we take out our anger or sadness on our loved ones. But we almost always feel remorse after having done this, and we rarely do it to hurt others. Anyone who wants you to feel bad because they feel bad is very dangerous, indeed. No matter how miserable you are, you never wish for your loved ones to suffer with you. Be very careful around someone who seems a little too comfortable allowing you to take on their emotional trials or burdens.

The Toxic Footprint (Sommer, n.d.)

Manipulators are still people, and people are creatures of habit. If you suspect someone of manipulating you, look for patterns of weird behaviour. Make a mental note every time you feel like something is wrong. What is the other person saying or doing? Do their words or actions match how you're feeling?

If someone is continually reminding you of "how much" they do for you, take a mental step back. Have they gone out of their way to be there for you? If someone is always making excuses for repeating the same bad behaviours, this is also a red flag. Unless the person is making a clear and distinct effort to correct their behaviour, a repeat offender is a manipulator. Someone who truly respects your boundaries and values their relationship with you will at least make an effort to change their behaviour if you communicate to them that something they've done or said is unacceptable.

It's Ok (Sommer, n.d.)

If someone did something that hurt you or made you uncomfortable, it's not ok. You can accept someone's apology or forgive someone without saying those words. "It's fine" or "it's ok" gives a manipulator permission to keep taking advantage of you. If you find yourself saying this a little too often, then it's time to re-evaluate your relationship with this other person. And if you find yourself saying this to someone who harmed you or intentionally put you in danger, then you should start trying to detangle yourself from that relationship emotionally.

You are... (Sommer, n.d.)

We've all said mean or cruel things, maybe in a fit of anger, or in a moment of insensitivity. But when someone is continually putting negative labels on you, then you're dealing with a manipulator. Remember, manipulators, thrive on guilt. The more you doubt yourself, your worth, and your abilities, the more emotionally dependent you are on them for love and approval. This makes you extremely vulnerable to their influence and allows them to control your attitudes and behaviours with the promise of respect and affection.

"You're a bad communicator," "you're not a very good cook," "you're ugly in red..." Every once in a while, a friend needs to give us some brutally honest feedback. But if the same person is continually assigning you negative labels, keep them at a safe emotional distance. No one deserves to have their self-esteem always knocked down. People who genuinely love you may say some mean things from time to time, but they will also let you know what your good qualities are. A manipulator will make you desperate for their praise, and sometimes even for their attention or affection. Don't let this happen to you. If you have to work to earn someone's love, then it's time to let them go.

STRATEGIES FOR DEFENCE

The ultimate defence against manipulators is the word 'no.' Being healthy and firm in your refusal to do anything that harms you or makes you uncomfortable virtually renders you manipulation-proof.

However, not all of us are so iron-willed, and skilled manipulators have a way of making even the most secure people concede to doing things that are against their best interests. When working with dark personalities, it can even be dangerous to advocate too strongly for yourself, especially if you have already established a relationship with that person. Short of laying healthy boundaries, there are a few other strategies you can employ to protect yourself from manipulators of all stripes.

Surround Yourself with Supportive People (Thibodeaux, 2020)

Isolation is the number one goal of a manipulative person. They will attempt to do this by sowing doubt in your mind (or even in the minds of your friends) – making you feel guilty about hanging out with your friends, telling you your friends are not good people, or even speaking badly about you to your friends.

Without other people around you, it becomes harder and harder for you to consider other options or hear other ideas. And of course, the less time you spend with others, the more time you spend with them, making it even easier for them to control you. Manipulators will never show their hand in front of others. Once they have been exposed as manipulative, they lose all their power. Maintaining strong relationships with supportive people is a natural defence against manipulators. If they are unable to isolate you, they will often leave you alone to find a more vulnerable target.

Remind Yourself of Your Goals and Priorities (Thibodeaux, 2020)

Your goals and priorities are not crucial to a manipulator. Their purpose is to influence you to do and believe what they want you to believe. If your personal goals and dreams come into conflict with theirs, then they will do everything they can to steer you away. Discouraging you from following your path can be as overt as telling you can't succeed, or as subtle as pressuring you to take projects that are far beneath your actual ability level.

Having clear life goals is healthy for every person, not the least because it protects you from people who will try to distract you from achieving them. Remind yourself every day of what your primary life goals are and be very wary of anyone who doesn't seem to support you achieving them. These don't have to be professional goals. Remind yourself of what kind of person you want to be, or what kind of lifestyle you want to have. When someone throws up logistical or relationship difficulties to stop you from achieving those things, you'll be able to see through them if you remain focused on getting what you truly want out of life.

Communicate Honestly Always (Thibodeaux, 2020)

Manipulators often try to convince you to do or say things that go against your genuine thoughts and wishes. The more you do this, the more power they have to control you. Manipulators don't only cause you to doubt yourself. Often, they will spread disinformation about you to other people that validate their version of who they want you to be. It can't be stated enough how receptive manipulators are to social validation. If they can't isolate you from your friends and family, then they will try to convince those around you that your 'true' self is the self that they want you to be. However, if you always maintain clear and honest communication with the people around you, this will become very difficult for a manipulator to do. The more you share and talk about yourself with your loved ones, the more control you have over the social narrative of who you are. The less you conceal from those who are close to you, the less power a manipulative person has to sway their opinion of you.

Call Them Out (Thibodeaux, 2020)

Manipulators tend to think that they're smarter than the people around them. They only employ their methods when they think they're not going to get caught. The moment they've been exposed, they lose their power over you. If someone is doing or saying something manipulative, don't be afraid to call them out. You don't necessarily have to use the word 'manipulative.' But if someone is doing something that makes you uncomfortable, tell them precisely what they're doing and how it makes you feel. If the other person denies the behaviour that you're complaining about, start writing things down, record days, times, and dates. Tell a close friend, family member, or romantic partner precisely what happened on the day of the encounter. Screenshot problematic text messages and emails. Once you've amassed enough proof, confront the manipulator again. When they realise that they aren't going to be able to trick you into trusting them again, they will often let you go and move on to another target.

Know Your Rights (Ni, 2014)

Manipulators dehumanise you. They attempt to strip you of your autonomy so that they can determine what you do and say. And they do this by making you believe that you don't deserve to be respected. Remember always that you have the right:

- to be treated with respect;
- to express your feelings, opinions, and wants;
- to set your priorities;
- to say 'no' without feeling guilty;

- to get what you pay for;
- to have opinions that are different from the opinions of others;
- to take care of and protect yourself from being threatened physically, mentally, or emotionally;
- to create your own happy and healthy life.

Anyone who makes you feel like you don't have the right to these things is manipulative. Anyone who makes you feel like you don't deserve these things does not have your best interests at heart.

CONCLUSION

Social influence is all around us. It's how marketers convince customers to buy their products and how businesses attract new customers. It's how teachers convince stubborn students to do their homework and how supervisors manage their employees. Social influence is how we compromise and how we communicate. It's the methods that we use to get what we want without instigating conflict. It's how we convince others to do what we want them to do when bluntly asking isn't respectful or appropriate.

However, there is a dark side to social influence. When the underlying psychological mechanisms of social influence are used to inflict harm on others, we call this manipulation. When someone is aware of those psychological mechanisms and uses them with ethical intent, however, we call this persuasion. They are two sides of the same coin, often employing similar methods but to very different ends.

Before you read this book, you may have been someone who found yourself always in conflict with other people. Perhaps you often got the label of 'difficult' or 'confrontational' for merely being clear about your wants and needs. With the help of the tactics in this book, you no longer have to endure the label of pushy or bossy. Rather than always fighting with others, you can employ simple strategies to convince others to do as you ask.

Or perhaps you were a bit of a wallflower. Perhaps you're someone who is easily cowed by others or afraid to speak up for what you want. With the help of these persuasive tactics, you no longer need to let opportunities pass you. A slight adjustment to your body language can help you to appear confident and attractive to others. Dr Cialdini's six weapons of persuasion can help you to get what you need from even the most difficult of people.

Or perhaps you're someone who is plagued by a dark and dangerous relationship. Perhaps there is someone in your life who isn't persuasive at all but is instead extremely manipulative. Whether this person has a dark triad personality type or is manipulative in less malicious ways, navigating a manipulative relationship can be utterly exhausting. Before you read this book, you may not have been sure what the real cause of your distress was. Perhaps you had your suspicions but were never quite able to catch your manipulator in the act. Now, not only do you have the tools you need to recognise a manipulative presence in your life, but you'll be able to employ some straightforward strategies to save yourself from their malignant influence.

Whether it's professional or personal, high stakes or a casual conversation, persuasion and manipulation are all around us. People are continually using persuasive tactics to get you to do as they ask. Though you may not realise it, you are also exerting a persuasive influence on other people. It's human nature. It's what we do. But there will always be those who try to use your human nature against you. Armed with the knowledge you now have, you'll never again find yourself tricked into doing anything against your will. Never again will you have to give up your autonomy to the whims of a malicious person or organisation. The time is now for you to take back control of your relationships. Say goodbye to manipulative people, and don't be afraid to use your social influence to get what you want out of life.

Thank you for reading my book. If you have enjoyed reading it perhaps you would like to leave a star rating and a review for me on Amazon? It really helps support writers like myself create more books. You can leave a review for me by scanning the QR code below:

Thank you so much.

Rebecca Dolton

ABOUT THE AUTHOR

 It's hard to find someone who isn't a little bit intrigued about psychology. Whether you have chosen it as your career or you want to learn more about yourself and others in your life, Rebecca Dolton allows us to explore dark psychology, neurolinguistics, and more in her book Beyond Persuasion.

Thanks to her background in psychology combined with her pure fascination for how the brain works and reacts to different stimuli, Rebecca Dolton has shown hundreds of people how to live better lives. She gently guides the reader with methods to improve their careers and develop stronger relationships.

Beyond Persuasion looks at how to influence people and how to handle manipulation to one's advantage. Her books also include how to quit drinking and how to rebuild your life once you have overcome the strong grip alcohol can take hold on you. The topic of getting back on track after traumatic events will also be one that will help change the lives of so many.

Reading Rebecca's books doesn't make you feel like someone is intruding. On the contrary, readers can feel safe exploring their thoughts and emotions. There is just the right amount of science to explain the concepts related to the mind but using a language that we can all relate to.

You feel safe.

REFERENCES

Amernic, J. H., & Craig, R. J. (2010). Accounting as a Facilitator of Extreme Narcissism. *Journal of Business Ethics*, *96*(1), 79–93. https://doi.org/10.1007/s10551-010-0450-0

Aronson, E., Wilson, T. D., Akert, R. M., & Sommers, S. R. (2015). *Social Psychology (9th Edition)* (9th ed.). London, United Kingdom: Pearson.

Asch, S. E. (1951). Effects of Group Pressure upon the Modification and Distortion of Judgments in H. Guetzkow (Ed.), Groups, leadership and men; research in human relations (p. 177–190). Carnegie Press.

Author, C. S. (2013, March 5). Haptics: The Use Of Touch In Communication. Retrieved from http://bodylanguageproject.com/the-only-book-on-body-language-that-everybody-needs-to-read/haptics-the-use-of-touch-in-communication/

Bandler, R., & Grinder, J. (1979). *Frogs Into Princes*. Amsterdam, Netherlands: Amsterdam University Press.

Bandler, R., Grinder, J., Satir, V., & Bateson, G. (2005). *The Structure of Magic, Vol. 1: A Book About Language and Therapy* (1st ed.). Palo Alto, California: Science and Behavior Books.

Battino, R. (2006). *Expectation*. New York, United States: Penguin Random House.

Beale, M. (2020, June 6). NLP Techniques List. 100+ Impressive NLP Methods. Retrieved from https://www.nlp-techniques.org/what-is-nlp/nlp-techniques-list/

BodyLanguageUniversity.com. (2019, January 19). The Human Voice - Part II Tone. Retrieved from http://www.bodylanguageuniversity.com/public/206.cfm

Brainwashing techniques vs mind control methods. (n.d.). Retrieved from https://www.decision-making-confidence.com/brainwashing-techniques.html

Brown, K. (2005). *Encyclopedia of Language and Linguistics* (2nd ed.). Amsterdam, Netherlands: Elsevier Science.

Cambridge Dictionary. (2020, June 3). manipulation meaning: 1. controlling someone or something to your own advantage, often unfairly or dishonestly: 2.... Learn more. Retrieved from https://dictionary.cambridge.org/us/dictionary/english/manipulation

Carter, G. L., Campbell, A., & Muncer, S. (2013). The Dark Triad Personality: Attractiveness to Women. *Elsevier/Science Direct*, 1–10. https://doi.org/10.1016/j.paid.2013.08.021

Clancy, F., & Yorkshire, H. (1989). The Bandler Method. *Mother Jones Magazine, 14*(2), 26–27.

Cooper, W. (2019). *Dark Psychology Secrets*. Seattle, Washington: Independently Published.

Corry, N., Merritt, R. D., Mrug, S., & Pamp, B. (2008). The Factor Structure of the Narcissistic Personality Inventory. *Journal of Personality Assessment, 90*(6), 593–600. https://doi.org/10.1080/00223890802388590

Covey, S., Tracy, B., & Hamilton, J. (2009). *Mission Impossible: Learn How to Reach Your Potential from Some of the World's Most Successful Possibility Thinkers*. Tennessee, United States: Insight Publishing.

Deutsch, M., & Gerard, H. B. (1955). A study of normative and informational social influences upon individual judgment. *The Journal of Abnormal and Social Psychology, 51*(3), 629–636. https://doi.org/10.1037/h0046408

Dilts, R. (1980). *The Study of the Structure of Subjective Experience*. California, United States: Meta Publications.

Ethics of Persuasion: Public Speaking/Speech Communication. (n.d.). Retrieved from

https://lumen.instructure.com/courses/218897/pages/linkedtext54304?module_item_id=5007183#:%7E:text=Ethics%20of%20Persuasion ,the%20knowledge%20of%20the%20audience.&text= For%20example%2C%20coercion%2C%20 brainwashing%2C,torture%20are%20never%20

considered%20ethical%20[1]

Experiential Constructivist Therapies Section. (n.d.). Retrieved from https://web.archive.org/web/20080612155128/http://www.psychotherapy.org.uk/experiential_constuctivist.html

Fremont College. (2018, March 8). How to Read Body Language - Revealing Secrets Behind Nonverbal Cues. Retrieved from https://fremont.edu/how-to-read-body-language-revealing-the-secrets-behind-common-nonverbal-cues/

Frick, P. J., & White, S. F. (2008). Research Review: The importance of callous-unemotional traits for developmental models of aggressive and antisocial behavior. *Journal of Child Psychology and Psychiatry, 49*(4), 359–375. https://doi.org/10.1111/j.1469-7610.2007.01862.x

Furnham, A., Richards, S. C., & Paulhus, D. L. (2013). The Dark Triad of Personality: A 10 Year Review. *Social and Personality Psychology Compass, 7*(3), 199–216. https://doi.org/10.1111/spc3.12018

Hall, E. T. (1990). *The Hidden Dimension (Anchor Books a Doubleday Anchor Book)* (First Paperback Edition). New York, New York: Anchor.

Horowitz, L. M., & Strack, S. (2010). *Handbook of Interpersonal Psychology: Theory, Research, Assessment, and Therapeutic Interventions* (1st ed.). New York, New York: Wiley.

Hurst, K. (2016, June 27). What Is NLP? 5 NLP Techniques That Will Transform Your Life. Retrieved from https://www.thelawofattraction.com/5-nlp-techniques-will-transform-life/

Jakobwitz, S., & Egan, V. (2006). The dark triad and normal personality traits. *Personality and Individual Differences, 40*(2), 331–339. https://doi.org/10.1016/j.paid.2005.07.006

Johnson, S. J. (1990). Enhancing human performance: Issues, theories, and techniques, edited by Daniel Druckman and John A. Swets. Washington, DC: National Academy Press, 1988. 299 pp., $32.50 cloth, $22.50 paper. *Human Resource Development Quarterly,*

1(2), 202–206. https://doi.org/10.1002/hrdq.3920010212

Jonason, P. K., Slomski, S., & Partyka, J. (2012). The Dark Triad at work: How toxic employees get their way. *Personality and Individual Differences, 52*(3), 449–453. https://doi.org/10.1016/j.paid.2011.11.008

Jones, D. N., & Paulhus, D. L. (2010). Different Provocations Trigger Aggression in Narcissists and Psychopaths. *Social Psychological and Personality Science, 1*(1), 12–18. https://doi.org/10.1177/1948550609347591

Kaufman, S. B., Yaden, D. B., Hyde, E., & Tsukayama, E. (2019). The Light vs. Dark Triad of Personality: Contrasting Two Very Different Profiles of Human Nature. *Frontiers in Psychology, 10*, 467–468. https://doi.org/10.3389/fpsyg.2019.00467

Kelman, H. C. (1958). Compliance, identification, and internalization three processes of attitude change. *Journal of Conflict Resolution, 2*(1), 51–60. https://doi.org/10.1177/002200275800200106

Kennedy, L. (2018, November 13). Inside Jonestown: How Jim Jones Trapped Followers and Forced 'Suicides'. Retrieved from https://www.history.com/news/jonestown-jim-jones-mass-murder-suicide

Klimstra, T. A., Jeronimus, B. F., Sijtsema, J. J., & Denissen, J. J. A. (2020). The unfolding dark side: Age trends in dark personality features. *Journal of Research in Personality*, *85*, 103915. https://doi.org/10.1016/j.jrp.2020.103915

Kohut, H. (2014). *The Restoration of the Self* (Reprint ed.). Chicago, Illinois: University of Chicago Press.

Kurien, D. (2010). Body Language: Silent Communicator at the Workplace. *IUP Journal of Soft Skills*, *4*(0.5), 29–36.
Retrieved from https://papers.ssrn.com/sol3/papers.cfmabstract_id=1610020#:~:text=Daisy%20N.,-Kurien&text=The%20role%20of%20body%20 20language,than%20any%20content%20delivered %20verbally.&text=But%2C%20body%20language%20-surpasses%20 all,invariably%20reveals%20the%20bare%20truth

Langford, J. M. (1999). Medical Mimesis: Healing Signs of a Cosmopolitan 'Quack.' *American Ethnologist*, *26*(1), 24–46. https://doi.org/10.1525/ae.1999.26.1.24

Louv, J. (n.d.). 10 Ways to Protect Yourself from NLP Mind Control. Retrieved from https://ultraculture.org/blog/2014/01/16/nlp-10-ways-protect-mind-control/

Mehrabian, A. (2009). "Silent Messages" - Description and Ordering Information. Retrieved from http://www.kaaj.com/psych/smorder.html

Milgram, S. (1963). Behaviour Study of Obedience. The Journal of Abnormal and Social Psychology, 67(4), 372-378. https://doi.org/10.1037/h0040525

Mondloch, C. J., Nelson, N. L., & Horner, M. (2013). Asymmetries of Influence: Differential Effects of Body Postures on Perceptions of Emotional Facial Expressions. PLoS ONE, 8(9), e73605. https://doi.org/10.1371/journal.pone.0073605

Ni, P. (2014, June 1). How to Spot and Stop Manipulators. Retrieved from https://www.psychologytoday.com/us/blog/communication-success/201406/how-spot-and-stop-manipulators

Paulhus, D. L., & Williams, K. M. (2002). The Dark Triad of personality: Narcissism, Machiavellianism, and psychopathy. Journal of Research in Personality, 36(6), 556–563. https://doi.org/10.1016/s0092-6566(02)00505-6

Petrides, K. V., Vernon, P. A., Schermer, J. A., & Veselka, L. (2011). Trait Emotional Intelligence and the Dark Triad Traits of Personality. Twin Research and Human Genetics, 14(1), 35–41. https://doi.org/10.1375/twin.14.1.35

Rauthmann, J. F. (2011). The Dark Triad and Interpersonal Perception: Similarities and Differences in the Social Consequences of Narcissism, Machiavellianism, and Psychopathy. *Social Psychological and Personality Science*, *3*(4), 487–496. https://doi.org/10.1177/1948550611427608

Robert B. Cialdini. (1984). *Influence: The Psychology of Persuasion, Revised Edition* (Revised ed.). New York, New York: Harper Business.

Rothmann, S., & Coetzer, E. P. (2003). The big five personality dimensions and job performance. *SA Journal of Industrial Psychology*, *29*(1), 29–30. https://doi.org/10.4102/sajip.v29i1.88

Simon, G. K. (2010). *In Sheep's Clothing*. Marion, Michigan: Parkhurst Brothers.

Sommer, E. (n.d.). How to Recognize and Protect Yourself From Manipulation. Retrieved from https://livepurposefullynow.com/recognize-and-protect-yourself-from-manipulation/

Sullivan, L. E. (2009). *The SAGE Glossary of the Social and Behavioral Sciences*. Thousand Oaks, Canada: SAGE Publications.

Thibodeaux, W. (2020, February 6). 4 Ways to Protect Yourself From Manipulative People. Retrieved from https://www.inc.com/wanda-thibodeaux/4-ways-to-protect-yourself-from-manipulative-people.html

Vernon, P. A., Martin, R. A., Schermer, J. A., & Mackie, A. (2008). A behavioral genetic investigation of humor styles and their correlations with the Big-5 personality dimensions. *Personality and Individual Differences, 44*(5), 1116–1125. https://doi.org/10.1016/j.paid.2007.11.003

Vernon, P. A., Villani, V. C., Vickers, L. C., & Harris, J. A. (2008). A behavioral genetic investigation of the Dark Triad and the Big 5. *Personality and Individual Differences, 44*(2), 445–452. https://doi.org/10.1016/j.paid.2007.09.007

Williams, T. (2011, June 26). Manipulation's Unethical Ethics. Retrieved from https://ecaminc.com/index.php/blog/item/255-manipulation-s-unethical-ethics#:%7E:text=Yes%2C%20positive%20context%20manipulation%20is,is%20ethical%2C%20manipulation%20is%20not.&text=As%20illustrated%2C%20ethics%20are%20societal,to%20next%20

its%20definition%20changes